P9-AQT-213

INCLUDES **DVD** VIDEO

KITCHEN CABINETS

MADE SIMPLE

WITHDRAWN

No longer the property of the Boston Public Library.
Sale of this material benefits the Library

GREGORY PAOLINI

The Taunton Press

Text © 2010 by Gregory Paolini
Photographs © 2010 by The Taunton Press, Inc., except where noted below
Illustrations © 2010 by The Taunton Press, Inc.
All rights reserved.

The Taunton Press

The Taunton Press, Inc., 63 South Main Street, PO Box 5506, Newtown, CT 06470-5506
e-mail: tp@taunton.com

Editor: Helen Albert, Castle Hill Media
Copy editor: Candace B. Levy
Indexer: Jay Kreider
Interior design: Susan Fazekas
Layout: Helen Albert
Illustrator: Christopher Mills
Cover photographer: Gregory Paolini
Photographers: Gary Junken © The Taunton Press, Inc., except as follows: p. 3 and 8, © Ken Gutmaker; p. 7 (top), © Eric Roth;
p. 7 (bottom), © davidduncanlivingston.com; p. 17 (bottom left), 19 (bottom), 43, 45, 46 (bottom), 67, 83, 84 (bottom), and
93 (bottom right), Gregory Paolini; p. 51 and 101 (top right), © Robert Settich; p. 69 (bottom), 71 (bottom), 84 (top left and top right),
88, and 119 (bottom right), Andy Rae

The following names/manufacturers appearing in *Kitchen Cabinets Made Simple* are trademarks:
Confirmat®, Emmy® Awards, Forstner®, KCMA®, Lee Valley Tools®, McFeely's™, Melamine®, Phillips®, Pozidriv®,
Rockler® Woodworking and Hardware, Woodcraft®, Woodworker's Hardware®, Woodworker's Supply®.

Library of Congress Cataloging-in-Publication Data

Paolini, Gregory.
  Kitchen cabinets made simple / author, Gregory Paolini.
      p. cm.
  Includes index.
  ISBN 978-1-60085-300-5
  1. Kitchen cabinets. I. Title.
  TT197.5.K57P36 2010
  684.1'6--dc22

                        2010036317

Printed in the United States of America
10 9 8 7 6 5 4 3 2 1

About Your Safety: Working wood is inherently dangerous. Using hand or power tools improperly or ignoring safety practices can lead to permanent injury or even death. Don't try to perform operations you learn about here (or elsewhere) unless you're certain they are safe for you. If something about an operation doesn't feel right, don't do it. Look for another way. We want you to enjoy the craft, so please keep safety foremost in your mind whenever you're in the shop.

acknowledgments

There are so many people that have a hand, either directly, indirectly, or unknowingly, in the creation of a book and video. It's a monumental project, which when done right, looks so simple. And while my name appears on the cover, it is the people acknowledged on this page that truly deserve recognition.

First and foremost, I'd like to express my most sincere gratitude to my wife, Mona. She is the love of my life and one of the driving forces for all that I do. She often remains in the background, taking no credit for all she does. I appreciate her patience and faith in me and especially her selfless sacrifices, which allow me to do what I love to do. Mona, this is for you!

Without the help of my editor, Helen Albert, this book would be nothing more than a bunch of notes cobbled together in a few dozen computer files. Helen, thank you for the expedited education as well as your insight into the publishing world. And more important, thank you for helping me take the leap into the world of books, without letting me land on my butt!

Special thanks to Courtney Jordan for production, and the Emmy® Award–winning Gary Junken, whose steady hand made the video easy to watch. To David Heim, whose sincere and candid advice has helped guide me on a glorious path; Rollie Johnson for enlightening and helping me figure out some of the things I'm still trying to figure out; and all the folks at *Fine Woodworking* magazine, who have helped me come this far.

Finally, I'd like to thank the rest of my family. Mom and Frank, the two of you have done so much to help make this dream come true, thank you! Gramma Choo-Choo, I hope I'm making you proud! And to my kids—Jaime, David, and Jenn—I love you all!

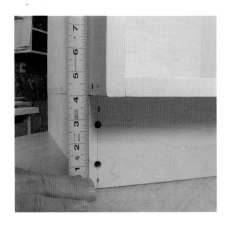
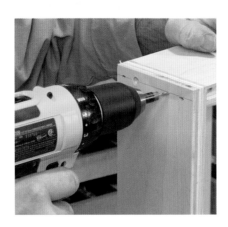

contents

chapter

1

Planning your project

The idea of building a kitchenful of cabinets can be a little intimidating, but the truth is, building an entire set of kitchen cabinets isn't that complicated. At its most basic level, a cabinet is essentially a large box, filled with more boxes, drawers and pullouts, and covered with slabs or panels (doors, drawer fronts, and finish panels). Although the construction process may be simple, there are ways to make the project go more smoothly.

There are many things to think about before you get started, ranging from what style to choose for your cabinets to where you will store the cabinet boxes while you're building them. In this chapter, I'll discuss the basics of planning and managing your project, including the standard dimensions for cabinets, the difference between frameless and face-frame cabinetry, the tools and materials you'll need for building your cabinets, and how to organize your work.

The first step in designing your kitchen is to figure out how you like to use it. In this kitchen, the cabinets were designed to include a computer work station as well as plenty of open shelving for books.

Making a plan

Before building any cabinets, you'll want to make a detailed plan with all the measurements for both the base cabinets and wall cabinets. The plan itself can be drawn on paper, but you'll also find many planning tools online or even at your local home center. These planning tools, whether electronic or paper-based, offer dimensions for standard commercial cabinets and can help you get started. Electronic versions allow you to try different scenarios. Some even allow you to see it in 3D. You can also use computer drawing programs, such as CAD or SketchUp.

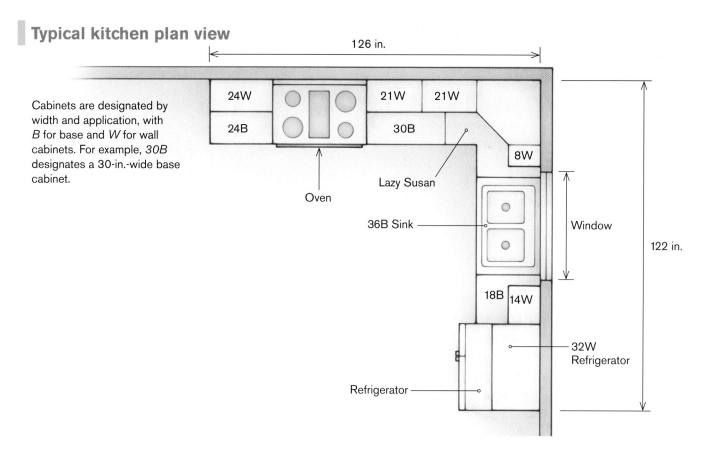

Cabinets are designated by width and application, with *B* for base and *W* for wall cabinets. For example, *30B* designates a 30-in.-wide base cabinet.

126 in.

24W

24B

Oven

21W   21W

30B

Lazy Susan

8W

36B Sink

Window

18B 14W

32W
Refrigerator

Refrigerator

122 in.

Before drawing your plan, think about how you use your existing kitchen. What do you like about it? What don't you like? Then, think about how to change the kitchen to suit your needs. Keep in mind that you may need to relocate the plumbing and electrical services if you move the sink, dishwasher, or stove.

Next, take your appliances into account, and make sure you leave room for them in your layout. Most manufacturers list overall dimensions or any clearances in their product literature. And even if you haven't purchased that stove, dishwasher, or refrigerator, you can most likely get a copy of the owner's manual and installation guide on the manufacturer's website.

You should draw both a plan view (from above) for the base cabinets and the wall cabinets. Be sure to note any window and doors as well as the location of the appliances. You can make some assumptions about the height and depth of the cabinets and the toekicks, which are same height for all the base cabinets. The following section provides some of the standard dimensions to keep in mind while drawing your plan.

Cabinet standards

Before you make the first cut or power up any tools, there are some standard sizes you'll want to work with when building cabinets. All these dimensions are based on ergonomics: the science of ideal dimensions for the way our bodies use practical objects like furniture, cabinets, and appliances.

Most of the standards outlined here have to do with height and depth. The width of a cabinet can vary within reason, but there are some issues to consider, including the number of doors for the space (see "Single vs. multiple doors," p. 85). A very wide cabinet is also more difficult to manage during installation. Last, and perhaps most important, be mindful of the proportions. You want the final dimensions to be pleasing to the eye as well as practical for storage.

Base cabinets

Base cabinets are generally 36 in. tall from the floor to the top of the counter. This distance off the ground puts the countertop at a comfortable working height. A little lower, and the average adult would have to bend slightly when chopping vegetables or prepping food at the workspace. In this hunched posture, you'd likely feel some back pain at the end of the day. If the cabinets were much taller, and you maintained the standard distance between the base and the wall cabinets, you'd have to stand on tiptoes to reach the contents of the upper cabinets. Appliance manufacturers also use 36 in. as their standard height, so that dishwashers, ovens, and cabinets will all align at the level of the countertop.

The depth of base cabinets is generally around 24 in. This really has more to do with materials than anything else. When you rip a 4-ft.-wide sheet of plywood in half, you end up with roughly two 24-in.-wide pieces that can be cut into cabinet sides and bottoms. You'll see in Chapter 4 that, depending on the sheet goods used, these pieces are not always exactly 24 in. wide, but you can adjust for the difference during construction.

Base cabinets sit on supports or toekicks, which are generally 4 in. tall and set back 3 in. from the front of the cabinet. This provides enough room to stand at the cabinet without stubbing your toes.

Countertops usually occupy the top 1½ in. of the overall height of the base cabinets. The actual thickness of the counters may vary, depending on the type of material chosen, so adjust accordingly.

Wall cabinets

Upper cabinets are roughly 12 in. deep. This width, as with base cabinets, is related to dimensions of standard materials. Theoretically, a 4×8 sheet of plywood yields four 12-in. sections across its width. Cutting the plywood reduces the width by the thickness of the sawblade, so the actual yield may be less than 12 in. But you can use the 12-in. depth as a rule of thumb. It also turns out to be a good size to store the items in the average kitchen and provides enough setback so the upper cabinets won't interfere with working at the countertop.

Upper cabinets are usually installed 18 in. above the countertop surface. This leaves plenty of room on the counter to work and enough space for small appliances, like coffee makers and mixers. It's also an easy reach when storing dishes and food items in the wall cabinets.

Standard cabinet dimensions

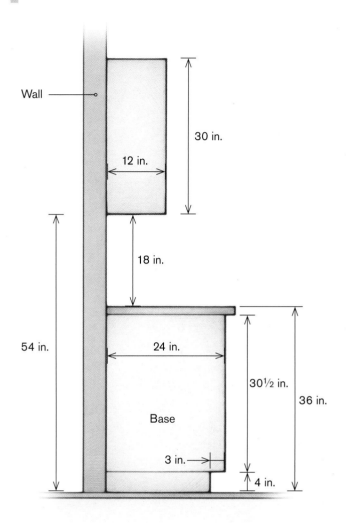

While there's no standard height for upper cabinets, a height of 30 in. is common. That's about as far as most people would be able to reach without the aid of something to stand on.

Depending on the height of the room and the style of the kitchen, the top of the cabinets can be trimmed with crown molding or left as is, providing space for additional display areas or interesting lighting effects.

Special cabinets

Building your own cabinets allows you many options that you wouldn't necessarily have with stock cabinetry. You may, for example, wish to build a cabinet in a narrow space at the end of a run to hold baking pans or cutting boards or build a closet for brooms and cleaning supplies.

One of the most common specialty cabinets is a corner cabinet. Specialty hardware can make it easier to access the contents of a corner cabinet.

Building corner cabinets is within the skills of most woodworkers. The key to success is careful attention to dimensions and angles. Be sure to understand the operation of the door hardware you plan for your corner cabinets. A base corner cabinet typically uses a folding door that operates on a special hinge, invisible when the door is closed. The installation is explained in detail in the instructions that come with the hinge.

Generally, it makes sense to plan ahead for all the hardware that you'll need for your cabinets. You don't want to get as far as installing the hardware to find out it doesn't work with your design. Especially be sure to plan for pullouts as they need to work with your door hardware (see "Accommodating pullouts," p. 102).

Building corner cabinets

Corner cabinets are a popular solution for using the dead space that is created where cabinets along adjacent walls meet. Corner cabinets can be filled with adjustable shelves or outfitted with a carousel or lazy Susan to make better use of the space. If your kitchen design will include a corner cabinet, familiarize yourself with any hardware that will be used for it before building the cabinet. Also, if you plan to have a face frame, make sure to deduct the thickness of the frame material from the width of the side that abuts the neighboring cabinet sides. The angle for the outside edge of the frame stiles is 22½ degrees so that the corner frame meets seamlessly with the frames of its neighbors.

It's important that you allow some space in the rear corner of the cabinet. Most kitchens don't have entirely plumb, square walls, and corners are notorious for buildup from drywall taping. Building in a back wall at a 135-degree angle gives you some extra clearance from the walls and won't diminish the storage space of the cabinet.

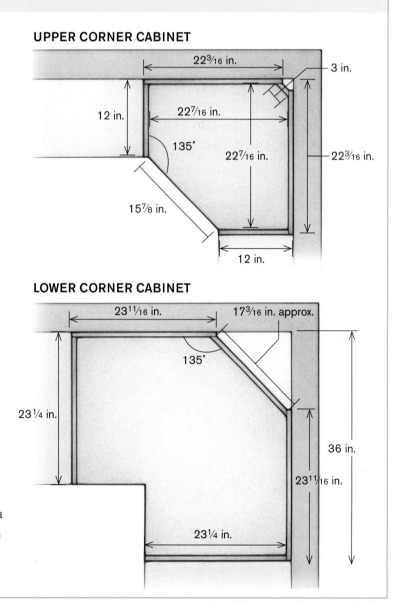

UPPER CORNER CABINET

LOWER CORNER CABINET

Traditional or Euro-style cabinets?

While there's an endless amount of cabinetry styles and themes to chose from, cabinets really break down into two types: traditional and frameless, or Euro-style.

Traditional cabinets

Often called face-frame cabinetry, traditional cabinetry gets its name from built-in shelving. As this primitive storage evolved to something more than just a shelf, construction usually involved trimming or framing in the area, to provide a method to attach doors and enclose the space. The frame also stiffened the cabinet box, giving it extra strength and providing a decorative transition. As the task of cabinet construction shifted from construction on site to the workshop, face-frame cabinetry persisted, especially for historic or period-style homes.

If you plan face-frame cabinetry, build the face frames first to the specifications dictated by your plan. Then build the boxes behind the frames.

A beaded frame around inset doors and drawers and period-authentic paint make these cabinets perfect for a colonial-style home.

These frameless cabinets have traditional frame-and-panel doors but are outfitted with specialty hardware, giving this contemporary kitchen an eclectic look.

The clean lines of these frameless cabinets work well in this contemporary setting.

Euro-style cabinets

Frameless cabinets made their debut in postwar Europe. Since Euro-style cabinets were, and still are, built modularly and, in Europe, are often moved from home to home, they need to be strong enough to survive the journey from the cabinet shop to the first home and then the next home. Sometimes the cabinet will be ganged together with other cabinets. Other times it will be solo. Since their inception, Euro cabinets were built as individual boxes, with thicker components, rendering the function of a face frame superfluous.

Many people associate Euro-style cabinetry with sleek contemporary designs, and while that's true in many cases, it's not the rule by any means. There are many ways to dress up Euro-style cabinets, so that they fit seamlessly into any environment. Outfitted with period-style doors and drawer fronts, a frameless cabinet can look appropriate even in a historical home.

So which type of cabinetry is stronger or better? Both styles of cabinets we cover in this book are built to accepted industry standards, and the truth is, once they're attached to your kitchen walls and locked together, neither type is going anywhere, and both will provide decades of service.

Euro-style = efficiency

By attaching a face frame to a cabinet, you gain a decorative element, but you eliminate a certain volume of usable storage space. The face frame overhangs by an inch on the outside, and ¼ in. on the inside of the box and on both sides, effectively decreasing the usable width of the cabinet by 2½ in.

Take that 2½ in. and multiply it by the average dimensions of a base cabinet box, or 30½ × 24, and you save 1,830 cu. in. for just one base cabinet. That's over a full cubic foot of storage space! Multiply that savings across a dozen or more cabinets in the entire kitchen, and you've just come up with enough storage space to fill a refrigerator.

Tools

It doesn't take a factory full of machinery to build a set of kitchen cabinets, but there are some basic tools you'll need to get the job done. Adding others will make the job easier and faster to complete. You can look at tools in terms of basic and preferred toolkits.

As part of your basic toolkit, you'll need a tablesaw. It doesn't have to be anything fancy, but it should be equipped with a quality combination blade and a reliable rip fence. Plus, you'll want to make sure it's stable enough to cut large sheets of plywood. This may mean investing in roller or support stands for stability. You'll also need a drill with various bits and drivers, a hammer, and a screwdriver. These are the basics, and you can get the job done if these tools are all you have.

For the preferred toolkit, or a well-equipped workshop, the tools and equipment I recommend are a router, a router table, a pocket-hole jig, a pneumatic stapler or nailer, a planer, a jointer, and a drill press. These tools make the job even easier, and you'll be able to tackle more options.

A tablesaw is invaluable for many cabinetmaking operations, from cutting cabinet parts to cutting tenons for door frames. Make sure that the blade is sharp and the rip fence and miter gauge are square to the miter slot.

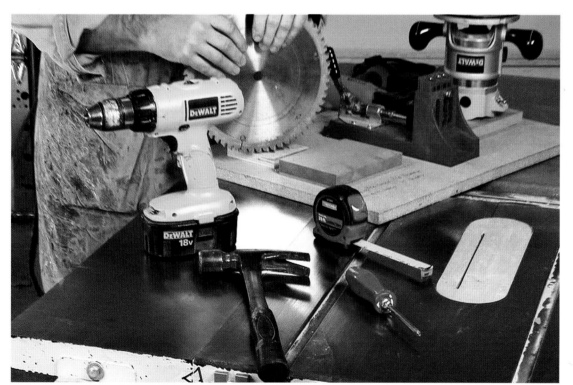

Some of the basic tools you'll need for building cabinets. Clockwise, from left: a portable drill, a sharp tablesaw blade, a pocket-hole jig, a router, an accurate measuring tape, screwdrivers, including any special drivers for hardware, and a framing hammer. Don't forget protection for your ears and eyes.

Make sure the plywood you choose has straight, even plies and relatively thick veneer on the faces. Thin exterior veneers sand through too easily.

Melamine gets it name from the laminate covering it. It's basically particleboard.

You'll have many choices for drawer slides and door hinges. I prefer standard, side-mount full-extension 100-lb.-rated slides and Euro-style adjustable cup hinges. But you can choose undermount slides (bottom) for some applications, and if you like the look of the hinge barrel on the outside of the door, you can use traditional hinges (top, center.)

Materials

The choice of materials is just as much a part of the design process as deciding on the dimensions of your cabinets and choosing the style of your doors and drawer fronts. The most important thing is to make thoughtful and timely decisions that have bearing on decisions you'll need to make later in the process, such as what type of door and drawer hardware you will use with face-frame cabinets. Here are some of the material choices to consider.

Sheet goods and solid wood

Kitchen cabinets are built from sheet goods, and by that I mean plywood or Melamine®. When buying plywood, look for straight and consistent layers in quality cabinet-grade plywood, preferably obtained from a plywood supplier. Avoid plywood with a wavy substrate and thin face veneers—it could warp, and the core can often show through the faces after finishing.

Melamine is just particleboard covered with a thin plastic coating, and it comes 1 in. oversize, so a 4×8 sheet is actually 49 in. by 97 in. It's less expensive than cabinet-grade plywood, and the slick white surface is easy to clean and reflects a lot of light in the inside of the cabinet. White Melamine can be found at select home centers. Other colors may be special ordered. Larger suppliers to cabinet shops often carry Melamine in patterns to resemble various wood species.

Although people talk about "solid-wood cabinets," it's actually impractical to use solid wood for cabinet boxes. Solid wood expands and contracts across its width throughout the seasons. Your kitchen cabinets are screwed to the studs in the walls and locked in place, offering no way to accommodate the wood's seasonal movement. It's best to save the solid wood for building doors and drawer fronts, where you can build in room for movement.

Hardware

One of the most important choices you'll make in the planning stage is the hardware that will make your cabinets functional. I prefer Euro-style hardware. It operates smoothly and installs easily and predictably. You'll also need fasteners, like staples or nails and screws, to

Make all the parts of a particular type (here, door frames) at the same time to avoid repetitive machine setups, but keep careful notes of dimensions for future reference. A consistent coding system helps identify parts when it comes time for assembly.

assemble the boxes, including 1⅝-in. wood screws (or drywall screws) and pocket-hole screws.

Make sure to order any specialty hardware, such as zero-protrusion or zero-clearance hinges for cabinets with pullouts that are near obstacles like appliances. Order corner cabinet hardware so that you can familiarize yourself with the hardware before finalizing the design.

Countertops

There are many countertop choices available: laminates, wood, tile, solid surface, stone, and even concrete. Different materials can vary tremendously in weight, which is a consideration. However, the cabinet construction covered in this book is based on time-tested standards and will be able to support most types of countertops.

Organizing your work

Cabinets take up a lot of room in the shop. Actually, an entire kitchen's worth of room. When I'm working on a large kitchen project, I sometimes cut all of the cabinet components and store them stacked in a pile in the corner of my shop. I hold off on assembly until just before installation. This allows me more room to work. It also makes finishing easier because I can work on flat panels rather than assembled casework.

There is a trade-off. You can end up with a lot of parts floating around, so it's essential to stay organized. Label all the components, and keep the parts for each cabinet stacked together. Keep the parts in an area where they won't be in the way or need to be moved.

Mark your parts as you work to keep track of what goes where.

I label all of the individual box components by their purpose—sides, bottom, nailers, stretchers—and I assign a cabinet designation to them. Examples are B33, for a 33-in.-wide base cabinet and W26 for a 26-in.-wide wall cabinet. When I'm sorting through the stack later, I'll know exactly which cabinet the part belongs to and where it goes.

Keep a careful log of measurements. This is especially helpful when it comes time to measure for drawers or doors. Without the assembled cabinet to measure, it's easy to make errors and, in turn, components won't fit right.

If possible, build and stack all the boxes until installation. That way you'll have the completed boxes for reference for measuring doors or drawers and a visual reminder of what still needs to be done.

If you can't fit all of the boxes in your shop, then you can always assemble them one by one and stage them in your garage, basement, spare room, or wherever they'll be out of the way for the duration of your project. If need be, you can even rent a small storage unit to keep clutter out of your house until your dream kitchen is done.

2

Building a
basic cabinet

K itchen cabinets are nothing more than a collection of boxes. Even drawers are basically simple boxes. So, the first thing to do is to learn how to make a basic box. Once you master this, you can customize the boxes, adding shelves, drawers, and pullouts as you choose.

Learning the basic construction and assembly methods will enable you to make both wall cabinets and base cabinets. While base cabinets and wall cabinets each have their own characteristics that make them specifically base or wall units, their construction is based on the same methods and layout.

In this chapter, you'll learn techniques for cutting pieces to size with consistent results, leaving clean edges that rival those made by professional cabinet shops. We'll also learn to groove parts, edge-band, and assemble a cabinet. So, let's gather up our materials and tools and head into the shop to build a basic cabinet box.

The first step in the construction process is to cut sheet goods into manageable pieces.

The process of building a basic cabinet

Like most projects in woodworking, building a box is much easier when you work in an organized step-by-step way. The overall process of building a box can be broken down into the following steps:

1. Cut plywood into manageable pieces.

2. Cut all the parts of the same kind to the same size.

3. Groove the sides, bottom, and top of the cabinet to hold the back panel.

4. Edge-band visible edges.

5. Assemble the cabinet, tacking the part in place with fasteners.

6. Countersink and drive screws to reinforce the joints.

Instead of wrestling a full-size sheet of plywood to the tablesaw, make the first cut with a circular saw. Before cutting, draw a line with a straightedge or T-square to ensure accuracy.

Cutting parts

The first step in building a cabinet is to break down a full-size plywood or Melamine sheet (usually a nominal 4 ft. by 8 ft.) into manageable pieces. I use a circular saw to make an initial crosscut at 32 in. This leaves me with partial sheets that are large enough to be used for cabinet sides or bottoms yet are light enough to maneuver safely and easily on the tablesaw.

I take the larger of the two partial sheets and crosscut it to 32 in. at the tablesaw. This leaves me with a total of three partial sheets at 32 in. Plus, I've maintained straight and square factory edges along two axes to use as reference for sizing components. If you have a smaller tablesaw, you may wish to cut off two pieces from the full sheet rather than try to manage the larger piece on a small saw table.

One of the keys to success in woodworking is consistency, and building kitchen cabinets is no different. Rather than measuring every part, measure one component and then set up to make every cut that needs to be made at that setting before you change the rip fence for a new width. That way, you're guaranteed that all of the parts will be exactly the same size.

Once you set your fence to cut parts to a certain dimension, cut all parts of that type before resetting the fence. This ensures that the parts will be consistent in size.

After making the initial cut, take the larger of the two partial sheets to cut at the tablesaw.

If you cut parts, then move the rip fence and come back later to reset it to the same measurement, in most cases you'll be off slightly from your original setting. While it won't seem like much, that small error will compound as you build the box, and you'll end up with a cabinet that isn't square and doesn't function properly. The doors and drawers won't open and close smoothly, and the cabinet will be difficult to square up with other cabinets in the run.

Grooving for the back

The back sits in a series of grooves let into the bottom, sides, and one of the top nailers. The easiest way to make this groove is by using a dado blade mounted in the tablesaw. You can also cut the groove with a standard sawblade. After cutting the first kerf, you reset the fence to make an adjacent, slightly overlapping cut. You'll continue this, widening the groove incrementally until you reach the desired width.

A router can also create grooves. A table-mounted router, outfitted with a ¼-in. straight bit, will cut clean consistent grooves. If you don't have a router table, you can use a handheld router mounted with an edge guide.

workSmart

When cutting sheet goods on the tablesaw, focus on the trailing edge of the rip fence. You want to make sure that the piece you're cutting always stays in contact with this area to ensure a high-quality parallel cut. Position your hands on the workpiece, making sure they will remain well clear of the blade during the cut, and practice the cut several times with the saw off and the blade lowered to get the hang of the process. For the best results and to reduce burn and saw marks, aim to slide the panel along the fence in one motion, without stopping.

Taming tearout

ven if you have a quality saw and it's tuned and in good working shape, tearout can occur when cutting solid wood or sheet goods, and it's most noticeable when cutting across the grain. But tearout is simple to tame as long as you consider its cause. Tearout happens for one reason: Unsupported wood fibers. That's why you'll see tearout where the blade exits the wood and there's no support.

Here are some of the methods for reducing or eliminating tearout at the tablesaw. Depending on the material you're cutting, you may use one method, or you may need to employ them all to achieve a high-quality cut free of tearout.

A. Choose the right blade. Be sure to use a sharp blade, one that's made for the material and the cutting operation you're performing. For general woodworking, I use a 40-tooth combination blade. It does a good job at ripping and cross-cutting hardwood. For cutting lots of plywood or Melamine, I turn to a triple chip blade. These blades have more teeth, with a less aggressive hook on the blade. The teeth are shaped to cut through fragile plywood veneers and Melamine coatings without damaging them.

B. Use a zero-clearance insert in your tablesaw. These replacement throat plates help support the wood fibers while you're cutting. They eliminate the gap

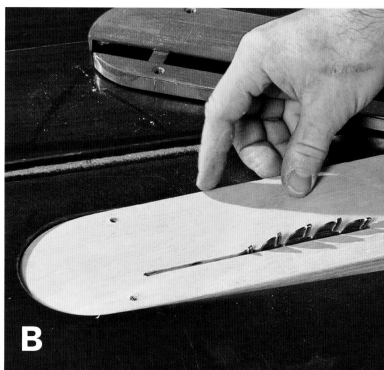

next to the sawblade. This gives extra support to the wood being cut on top of it and helps reduce tearout. You can buy an aftermarket commercial insert or make one from scrap plywood.

C. Make scoring cuts by raising the blade about $1/16$ in., just high enough to cut through the first layer of veneer or Melamine. Make an initial pass on the saw to score the piece, then raise the blade to the proper height to make a through cut, and take a second pass. Scoring takes extra time, because you essentially make double the number of cuts, but it's a very effective method of reducing tearout. This method is so effective, that many high-end cabinet shop saws come from the factory with a secondary scoring blade installed in them. It allows the operator to score and cut in a single pass.

D. Apply a piece of painter's tape on the back side of the area where you'll make your cut. The tape will help keep the fibers together by spreading the stress of the cut and exiting blade across a wider area. Just be sure to use painter's tape which releases easily. Standard masking tape and other types of tape that have too much adhesive power will cause their own tearout problems when removed. Some tapes have such powerful adhesives that they'll tear the veneer right off.

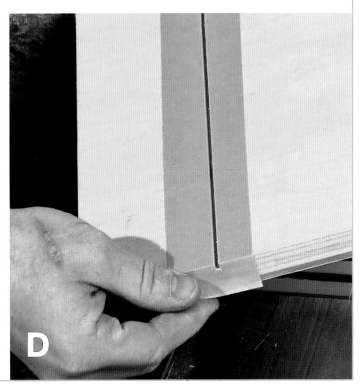

Edgebanding is faced on one side with heat-activated glue. Banding tape made of real wood veneers comes in a variety of common species. There is also edgebanding tape for Melamine.

Edgebanding

Before assembling the cabinet box, you'll want to cover the exposed edges of the plywood or Melamine. You don't want to see these raw edges on a finished cabinet, and it's much easier to cover them up before you assemble the cabinets. I cover any edge that will be left exposed and visible in the finished cabinet. This usually means all of the front facing edges, but you may also want to cover edges of the tops and bottoms of the sides as well, because depending on where the cabinet is located, those edges may be visible too. This will also apply to shelves and partitions on the inside of the cabinet.

For most of my edgebanding operations, I reach for preglued edgebanding tape. This tape has heat-activated adhesive applied to the back. You can get it in many colors and a variety of wood grains to match the material you're using to build your boxes.

workSmart

Adding solid wood banding to the front edge of the cabinet increases the depth of each component. Be sure to reduce the depth of components by ¾ in. when banding with solid wood.

If the edge of your cabinet will be left open, or exposed to a lot of abuse, you may want to consider applying solid wood to the edges. Solid-wood edgebanding is more durable than the tape banding but requires significantly more work to complete. You can see how I do solid-wood edgebanding, which can also be used to reinforce shelving, on p. 26.

Assembly

All of the joints in the cabinet are simple butt joints, reinforced with screws. It may not seem like a very strong joint, but the screws actually act like little tenons, and their sheer strength is incredibly high, making for a joint that's stronger than the material surrounding it. Plus, this method is based on an industry standard for custom cabinetry.

To keep the parts steady as you drill, countersink, and drive the fasteners, you could clamp the cases together, but I find it easier and faster to tack the parts together with 1¼-in.-long staples. This isn't a structural joint, but just like a clamp, it just keeps the parts from moving around during assembly. A brad nailer or finish nailer would work as well.

After tacking the corners of the box together with staples, reinforce the joints with screws.

Alternative joinery options

You don't have to rely on drywall screws for the strength of your cabinets. There are a number of joinery options that work equally as well or even surpass the strength of a joint reinforced with drywall screws.

Biscuits are small compressed pieces of beech hardwood in the shape of a football. When biscuits come in contact with moisture or yellow glue, they swell, tighten-ing the joint. The biscuits are inserted into a mortise cut with a biscuit joiner, or plate joiner. The joiner is simple to use, although orienting the joint for a flush fit does require some practice. Biscuits are a good choice when the outside of a cabinet will not be covered by a panel and you don't want to see any fasteners.

Rabbets create a classic woodworking joint and excel at positioning a component exactly where you want it. When used with solid wood in a long-grain to long-grain orientation, the rabbet is incredibly strong. When used with sheet goods for cabinetry applications, the rabbet needs to be reinforced with a mechanical fastener to ensure a joint strong enough to last.

Dowel joinery lends itself to commercial cabinet shops, where large automated machines perform most of the machining operations. While there are jigs available to perform dowel joinery on a small scale, most small shops have embraced biscuit joinery as a quicker alterna-tive. Like biscuits, dowels offer a very strong joint when you don't want to see fasteners on the outside of the cabinet.

Confirmat® screws are a cross between a dowel and a screw and provide a very strong joinery solution. Installing Confirmat screws require a special drill bit able to drill the bore for the screw portion and the dowel portion in one quick operation. According to commercial cabinet industry standards, Confirmat screws are consid-ered the strongest joinery option.

From left to right: biscuit joint, rabbet joint, dowel joint, and Confirmat screws.

Cutting sheet goods down to rough size

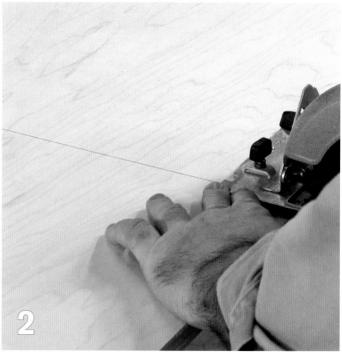

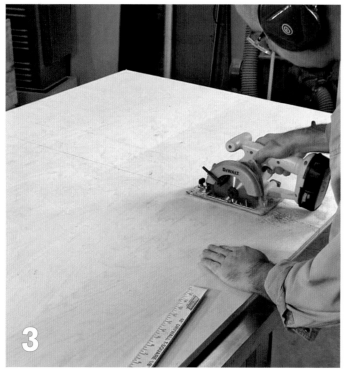

Start your project by rough cutting full sheets of plywood or Melamine into manageable sizes. The easiest way to do this is with a circular saw and a tablesaw.

1. **Measure off 32 in.** from the top factory edge and mark with a T-square.

2. **Line up the outside edge** of the cutting guide with your mark.

3. **Cut the sheet, following the guidelines,** until approximately the halfway point.

4. **Clamp the cut edge** across the saw kerf to prevent it from flopping open during the cut. Continue the cut from the opposite side.

5. **Take the larger of the two partial sheets** to the tablesaw and set the rip fence to 32 in.

6. **Cut the sheet to a width of 32 in.** This leaves you with a total of three partial sheets at approximately 32 in. in width. Plus you've maintained straight and square factory edges along two axes to use as reference for sizing components.

7. **Mark the factory edges** and tablesaw cut with a light-colored chalk for future reference.

Cutting cabinet parts to size

When cutting the sheets into their final sizes, it's important to consider the cutting sequence so that all parts are cut to consistent size. Since cabinet sides are the same height across the run (although different heights for base or wall cabinets), it's best to begin by cutting all the sides to height.

1. **Adjust the fence for the depth of the cabinet.** Make all cuts that need to be made at this measurement. In this case, the sides and the bottom, which will be cut to depth. After this step, you will have sides that are completed and a bottom that is cut to depth.

2. **Cut the bottoms to length.** The other parts of the cabinet, which are the same length as the bottom, are the nailers and stretchers. After cutting the bottom, cut the plywood panels you set aside for the nailers and stretchers to length.

3. **Rip the nailers and stretchers** to the same width, usually 4 in.

4. **Cut the back panel** from ¼-in.-thick sheet goods to match the rest of your cabinet. The final size of the back panel should be ½ in. wider than the bottom and 1 in. shorter than the sides in order to fit into the grooves that will be cut to hold it.

workSmart

Following a planned cutting sequence will ensure that the parts are consistent and your cabinets are square.

1. Cut the sides to height.
2. Cut the sides and bottom to depth.
3. Cut the bottom, nailers, and stretchers to length.
4. Cut the nailers and stretchers to width.
5. Cut the back panel to size.

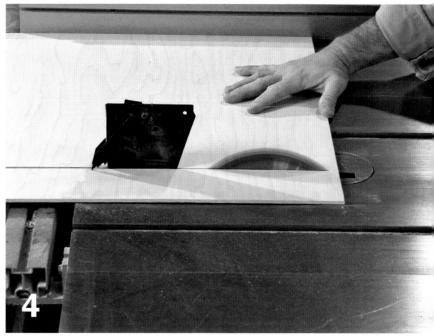

Grooving with a dado blade

The back sits in a series of grooves let into the bottom, sides, and one of the nailers. The easiest way to make this groove is with a dado blade at the tablesaw.

1. **Install a ¼-in. dado blade** into the tablesaw.

2. **Raise the height of the blade** just a hair over ¼ in., which leaves a little wiggle room for the back panel during assembly.

3. **Adjust the rip fence,** finding the distance by placing one of the stretchers between the fence and the dado blade. That's the exact distance from the back edge of the side and the bottom to groove.

4. **Cut the grooves** on the back edge of both inside faces of the sides, the bottom, and one of the stretchers.

Grooving with a standard tablesaw blade

Don't have a dado blade? No worries. You can cut the grooves using a few different methods, and the results will be exactly the same. Here, I'm using a zero-clearance insert, which helps reduce tearout.

1. **Set the blade height** and rip fence using the same method described in steps 1 and 2 on the facing page. Make a single pass on each piece.

2. **Adjust the rip fence,** adding the kerf width of the blade you're using, and make another series of passes.

3. **Repeat step 2** until the back panel fits into the groove.

Edge-banding with iron-on tape

Use a dedicated iron just for edgebanding. Some of the glue from the tape will work its way onto the face of the iron. If you return it to the laundry, the glue will end up on your clothes.

1. **Set the iron to medium,** often the polyester setting.

2. **Tear off a piece of tape** a couple inches longer than the component you're going to band, and center it over the edge.

3. **Work the iron along the edge.** The first pass with the iron holds the tape in place. Move the iron 3 in. or 4 in. per second for the initial pass. Reducing your speed by about half, work your way back, letting the glue really melt and adhere.

4. **Burnish the tape** with a block of wood immediately after ironing, while the glue is still active. Rub the block back and forth along the entire length, pressing down flat to seat the tape. After about a half dozen flat passes, angle the block slightly, then apply pressure to the edges for another half dozen passes.

5. **Trim the tape to length** with a razor blade, scoring it from underneath and snapping it off from above. Use the burnishing block as a surface to score against. Tilt the block after the scoring cut, and the banding will usually break right off.

6. **Trim the banding to width** with an edge trimmer. I make one pass in each direction with the trimmer for best results.

7. **Ease the sharp edge** by taking a few passes with 150-grit sandpaper. You're done when the edges feel friendly to the touch.

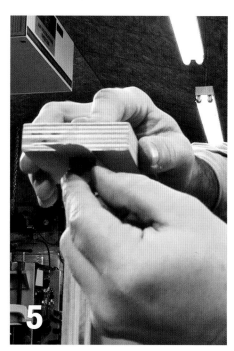

5

6

7

Assembling the cabinet

With all of the components cut to size and edgebanding applied to exposed edges, you're ready to begin the assembly process.

1. **Mark the side panels** on the outside faces, along the top, back, and bottom edges, with guidelines ⅜ in. from the edge. This will place the fasteners in the center of the ¾-in. edge of the mating component.

2. **Line up a side and the bottom** and tack them together. Any minor alignment issues will show at the back of the cabinet, but since that side is against the wall and covered, any offset will be hidden.

3. **Repeat the process** on the other side. Use a bench dog as a stop to keep the cabinet from sliding around during assembly. A block of wood clamped to the benchtop also works.

4. **Roll the cabinet onto its top,** and place the front stretcher in position. The benchtop acts as a reference surface and locates the front stretcher in line with the top edges. Tack the stretcher in place with a few staples.

5. **Set the cabinet upright** and slide the back into the grooves, making sure it's well seated and the top edge of the panel is about ½ in. from the top of the cabinet.

6. **Fit the rear stretcher** into position and align it with the top and back edges. Secure the rear stretcher with staples.

7. **Install the two nailer strips.** Press them against the back to seat the back panel against the grooves. This will help eliminate any gaps seen on the inside of the cabinet. A couple staples help hold the nailers in place.

8. **Install screws** to make the joints structurally sound. Place the cabinet box on the floor, laying on its side. Drill and countersink a series of holes, then drive in #6 by 1⅝-in. coarse-thread drywall screws. Use two screws at each stretcher or nailer. On the bottoms, use five screws for a base cabinet and three screws for a wall cabinet. Flip the cabinet over, and repeat the process to finish up the assembly.

Combination drill and countersink bits allow you to perform two drilling operations at one time. They are available in sizes for most screws and can be found through many woodworking suppliers and home centers. If your drill/driver has an adjustable clutch, set it to limit the amount of torque imparted on fasteners. Stay a good inch from the corner to avoid splitting the material when driving screws.

Building base cabinets

B ase cabinets are the foundation of your kitchen cabinetry project. They are the largest cabinets in the kitchen and provide the bulk of the storage area. Because they are such a dominant element in a kitchen, the base cabinets and their finish panels, drawer faces, and doors establish the style and overall feel of the room. Base cabinets also provide support for the countertop, where food preparation and other kitchen tasks take place. It's even possible to have a kitchen composed of base cabinets, without a single wall cabinet, if it suits your style. While I'm writing this book, I'm building just such a kitchen.

In this chapter, we'll look at determining the sizes for the components that will make up the base cabinets. We'll address some of the common concerns you may encounter when building base units and a few dilemmas that you may encounter, depending on the materials you choose. Plus, we'll look at a number of ways to build the toekicks to support the base cabinets.

A base cabinet consists of a basic cabinet mounted on a toekick. In this cabinet, a stretcher defines the drawer opening.

Dimensioning base cabinets

The standard height for base cabinets is 36 in., which includes a 1½-in.-thick countertop and a 4-in.-tall toekick. Subtract those two measurements, and you are left with a cabinet box that's 30½ in. tall. So, the two sides will be cut at a length of 30½ in.

The standard distance from the front edge of a base cabinet box, or carcase, to the rear edge is 24 in., making the two sides 30½ in. high by 24 in. deep. The depth of the bottom of the cabinet will be 24 in. as well.

In theory, you can get two 24-in. cabinet sides from a 48-in.-wide plywood panel, but in reality, you need to account for the material wasted by the saw kerf. For most sawblades, this waste is about ⅛ in. per cut. If you're building your cabinets out of Melamine, which is oversize by 1 in., there's no problem. A full sheet of Melamine is 49 in. wide, giving you plenty of margin for the saw kerf. If you're planning to build face-frame cabinets, the width of a standard sheet of plywood is not an issue because

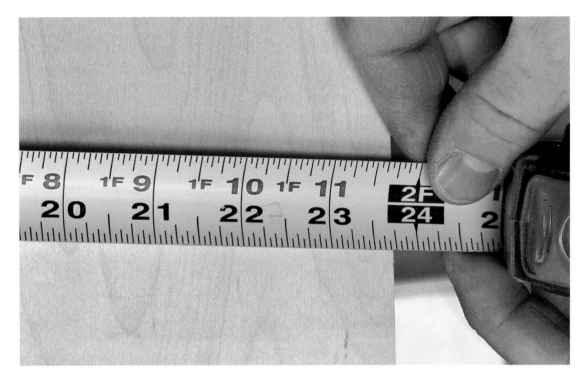

The standard for base cabinets is 24 in. deep, but you can get only two 23¾ in. sections out of a standard 4×8 sheet of plywood. Fortunately, this won't affect the performance of the cabinet.

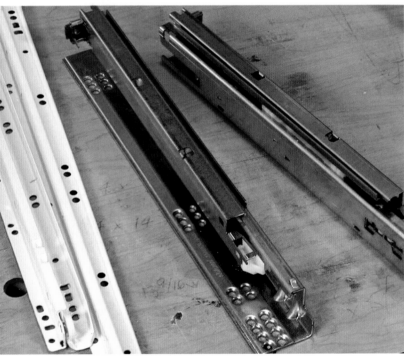

The industry standard for drawer slides is 22 in. so a cabinet with 23¾-in. sides will accommodate the slides with no interference in their operation.

you'll reduce your cabinet sides by ¾ in. to accommodate the face frame's thickness.

So how do you cut the sides from cabinet plywood without wasting material? The simple solution is just to make your cabinets 23¾ in. deep. That missing ¼ in. won't be noticed, and it won't interfere with anything inside of the cabinet. The industry standard for drawer slides and runners in base cabinets is 22 in. in length. Starting with a 23¾-in. depth, subtract ¾ in. from the depth for the thickness of the rear stretchers, and ¼ in. for the thickness of the back panel, which leaves you with 22¾ in., plenty of room for the 22-in.-long hardware.

On occasion, you may need to match existing cabinets or flank an object or appliance that requires a particular depth, which means you may need to make a 24-in.-deep cabinet. If you encounter one of these scenarios, or if you just really want 24-in.-deep cabinets, there are solutions. (See the sidebar on the facing page.)

Cabinet width is dictated by your needs or design requirements. That's one of the great things about building your own kitchen cabinets. If you want a cabinet that's 19¹³⁄₁₆ in. wide, you can build it to that width. So you get to decide how wide you want all of your boxes, but keep in mind that there are some common sizes or ratios that just look good to us. Most of the cabinets I build are 24 in. to 36 in. wide. And it's easier to work in whole numbers than trying to figure out lots of fractions. I try to avoid cabinets wider than 36 in. because of span and support issues, plus doors and drawers for cabinets any wider look awkward. Never mind trying to get a too-wide cabinet through doors once it's built!

workSmart

Plywood and Melamine are generally sold with a nominal indicator—for example, ¾ in. thick, ½ in. thick, etc. In reality, the actual thickness varies, depending on the type of material and the country of origin. Always measure your sheet goods to know exactly how thick they are, and adjust your cut list accordingly.

Achieving a 24-in. depth with standard plywood

If you're building a base cabinet with plywood, and your design or application requires a 24-in.-deep cabinet, you have several options available to achieve the desired depth.

Use a solid-wood edgeband. A piece of ¾-in.-thick hardwood applied to the front edge of the panels effectively increases the depth of the cabinet. In addition, it provides a more durable edge treatment.

Apply a ¾-in. back. Eliminate the ¼-in. back panel, its corresponding grooves, and the two rear stretchers, then apply a ¾-in.-thick back panel to the rear of the cabinet. This method provides a much stronger back and increases the overall depth of the cabinet by ¾ in. More information on applied backs can be found in Chapter 4.

Shim the rear of the cabinet. If the interior depth is less critical than the exterior depth, just tack on some strips of ¼-in. plywood to the back portion of the cabinet to shim it out to 24 in. deep.

Add a face frame. Changing from Euro-style cabinets to face-frame cabinets adds an additional ¾ in. of material in front of the cabinet box. Face-frame cabinetry is covered in depth in Chapter 5.

A face frame will provide the extra ¾ in. of depth if you want to build base cabinets to a full 24 in. using standard plywood sheets. Face frames have the added benefit of providing rigidity to the cabinet boxes but require more work to install drawer slides and hinges.

For Euro-style cabinets (frameless), you'll need to add a stretcher to the cabinet box wherever a drawer meets a drawer or a door. In face-frame cabinets, the stretchers are part of the fame.

When planning cabinet widths, take into consideration the space for slides for special features like pullouts for pots or pantry storage.

To size the bottom, as well as all of the nailers and stretchers, take the desired cabinet width and subtract two times the cabinet box material's thickness. Don't rely on the nominal designation; be sure you measure the exact thickness of whatever material you use.

Customizing base cabinets

If you're building Euro-style cabinets and plan to incorporate a bank of drawers in a cabinet or combine a drawer with doors, you'll need to cut additional stretchers. These stretchers will be used to separate the drawers from one another or from the doors. The stretcher also gives the doors something to close against.

You'll need an extra stretcher everywhere a drawer meets another drawer or a door. For example, on a base cabinet with a bank of four drawers, you will need three extra stretchers to act as dividers or separators.

Cut the extra stretchers at the same time you cut the rest of the nailers and stretchers for the cabinet. And be sure to edge-band the front edge, as these stretchers will be visible from the outside of the cabinet.

The toekick is usually about 4 in. in height. This is just about the right height to get close enough to the cabinet while fitting your toe underneath.

If you plan to use face frames on your cabinets, don't worry about the extra stretchers. The medial stiles of the face frames will act as a partition separators. (Face frames are covered in Chapter 5.)

Toekicks

A toekick is simply a recessed base that supports the base cabinets. Without the recess, your feet would bang against the doors or drawers when you stand close to the cabinets. Vacuum cleaners and brooms would scar the fronts of the cabinets during regular household cleaning.

Simple toekicks provide support for the cabinet, raising it up above the floor and providing a place for feet. The generous reveal also adds visual appeal.

There are several methods for making toekicks. Integral toekicks require cabinet sides to be 34½ in. long, but you can get only two sections of that length from a sheet of plywood. If your cabinet sides are cut to a length of 30½ in., as for an applied toekick, you can get three. Applied toekicks conserve material by allowing you to make use of remnants and offcuts. Integral toekicks require precise cuts in the cabinet sides, but applied

toekicks are constructed with simple butt joints, requiring only rip cuts and crosscuts. An applied toekick is easily attached to the cabinet with pocket-hole screws or biscuit joinery.

Pocket screws provide a quick, secure connection between the toekick base and the cabinet box.

Building a base cabinet

Building a base cabinet is just a minor variation of building the basic box shown in Chapter 2. Following the basic box strategy, cut the parts to size. Side panels will be 30½ in. high, and the depth depends on the materials and options mentioned earlier. The bottom will be the same depth as the sides. The nailers, stretchers, and bottom are sized roughly 1½ in. less that the cabinet's overall width. Remember to check the thickness of your materials to get an exact measurement. If you're off by $\frac{1}{16}$ in. here, it will compound to ¼ in. in just four cabinets.

1. **Cut all parts to size** following the basic box cutting strategy. Cut the sides to height, cut the sides and bottom to depth, cut the bottom and nailers and stretchers to length, and cut the nailers and stretchers to width.

2. **Groove the parts** for the back on the cabinet sides, bottom, and rear stretcher.

3. **Apply edgebanding** or solid wood to any edges that will be visible after installation of the cabinet.

4. **Assemble the cabinet,** tacking the parts as you go. Start by attaching one side to the bottom, then attach the second side to the bottom. Slide the back into the groove and then attach the top stretchers.

5. **Turn the cabinet on its face** and tack the nailers.

6. **Reinforce the joints** with #6 by 1⅝-in. coarse-thread drywall screws. First, drill and countersink for the screws. Place five screws along each side of the bottom and two screws on each side for every nailer or stretcher. Use your drill's clutch feature to avoid driving the screws too deep.

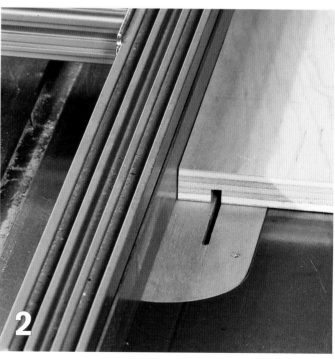

Installing partition stretchers

In cabinets without a face frame, you need to install a stretcher to divide drawers from one another or to separate a drawer from a door. Cut all stretchers for a cabinet to length at the same time to ensure that the cabinet will remain square and the cabinet sides will fit snugly.

1. **Make spacers** from scrap plywood the exact height of the drawer opening. Clamp a spacer tightly against the top stretcher on both sides of the cabinet.

2. **Position the stretcher** within the cabinet, making sure it is tight to the spacer and flush to the cabinet front.

3. **Mark the center** of the stretcher edge, using a square.

4. **Drill and countersink** for #6 by 1⅝-in. coarse-thread screws, and drive two screws on each side of the stretcher.

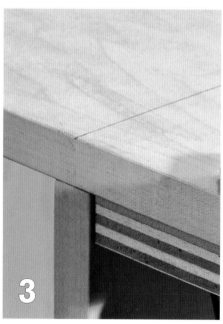

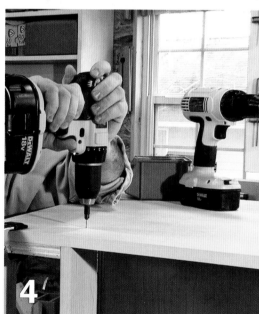

Cutting parts for toekicks

A simple applied toekick can be made from remnants or scraps of ¾-in. plywood. This has the advantage of making good use of materials.

1. **Rip lengths of ¾-in. plywood** into 4-in.-wide pieces. This will represent the height of the toekick, providing plenty of room for a foot to fit under the cabinet box and raising the box up to the 34½-in. mark, where the counter-top begins.

2. **Crosscut the 4-in.-high strips** to length. You'll need two pieces that are the overall width of the cabinet and two that are 19½ in. long. This measurement will provide a 3-in. setback from the face of the cabinet once the toekick is assembled and attached.

3. **Mark the inside faces** of the parts for easy reference when cutting pocket holes and assembling the toekick.

workSmart

When cutting plywood for toekicks, don't worry about grain direction. After installation, you'll cover all of the individual toekicks with a strip of ¼-in. plywood, making them look like one long seamless base.

Drilling pocket holes

Drill for pocket screws along one edge of each piece to provide for an easy method for attaching the toekick. Holes should be drilled every 6 in. to 8 in. for maximum strength. Make sure the stop collar on the drill bit is set for drilling ¾-in. material. (For more on drilling pocket holes, see p. 57.)

1. **Clamp the workpiece** in the pocket-hole jig with the inside of the component to be drilled facing you. Align the mark on the jig with layout lines you've drawn to indicate the position of the fasteners.

2. **Drill** until the stop collar reaches the top of the guide bushing. (You may need to back out to clear some of the chips before you reach full depth.)

workSmart

By using a shopmade angled block with an indexing fence and chucking up a ⅜-in. Forstner® bit in a drill press, you can drill pocket holes without investing in a proprietary jig. You'll need to drill pilot holes before driving the screws.

Other ways to attach toekicks

Tabletop fasteners (also known as figure eights) or desktop fasteners will hold the toekick to the cabinet. Recess the fasteners into the top of the toekick by drilling shallow holes along the top edge of the toekick with a ⅞-in. Forstner bit.

Biscuits do a fine job of holding toekicks onto the cabinets. If you use biscuits, don't glue them in until installing the cabinets, in case you need to make any adjustments for plumbing or HVAC.

Assembling a toekick

The trickiest part of assembling pocket-screw components is making sure all the pocket holes are on the interior and aligned in the same direction.

1. **Mark a guideline** on the end of each piece to indicate where to predrill and countersink.

2. **Arrange the components** so that all the pocket holes are on the inside and facing in the same direction.

3. **Make sure the corner aligns** and is flush top and bottom, and tack it with 1¼-in. staples. Continue tacking the corners around the perimeter of the box.

4. **Reinforce the corner joints** with #6 by 1⅝-in. coarse-thread drywall screws. Drive two screws at each end.

workSmart

If your cabinets will be resting directly on concrete when installed, use pressure-treated plywood to build the toekicks. It resists moisture issues associated with concrete slabs much better than standard plywood.

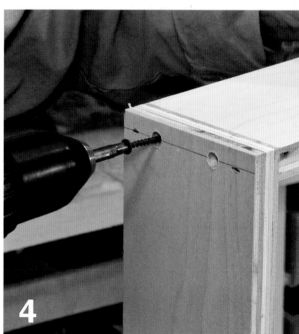

Attaching toekicks

If you've been careful to keep your toekick square, attaching it to the base with pocket screws is easy and fast.

1. **Align the toekick,** making sure it is flush to the rear of the cabinet.

2. **Drive screws** in opposite diagonals to secure the toekick to the cabinet base.

3. **Finish with the center screw** on each component. Check to make sure all screws are seated properly and the toekick is tight to the base.

❲workSmart

Adjust the clutch on your drill so that it just seats the screw at the bottom of the pocket hole.

Other ways to build toekicks

There are a number of other ways to support your cabinets and provide toekick clearance at the same time. Here are some other methods I've used, depending on the installation site and requirements.

Plywood base with fastening stretchers. This was the base used by many cabinetmakers before the widespread availability of pocket screws. It's essentially made the same way as the applied base but with two extra pieces cut to the 19½-in. length. These extra pieces are attached horizontally at the top of the kick and serve as flanges, so the assembly can be secured to the cabinet from the inside, using 1¼-in. screws.

If you have multiple adjacent cabinets, you can make an extra-long version on this style kick to support all of the cabinets on one assembly. This toekick is relatively lightweight and can be installed and leveled on site with ease; set the cabinets on top and fasten in place.

2×4 base. A quick base can be made from 2×4 construction lumber. This yields a toekick that is 3½ in. high. It can be shimmed up a little during installation, to achieve a 4-in.-high toekick. Use pressure-treated lumber if installing the cabinets directly on concrete.

Blocking base. Glue and clamp two 2×4 studs face to face, then crosscut the glued-up studs at 4-in. lengths to make block supports. The blocks are secured to the cabinet from inside by drilling and countersinking for two 2½-in.-long screws per block. Install the blocks at the front outside edges of the cabinet, on a line drawn 20 in. from the front edge. Install a second set of blocks at the rear corners and then spaced or centered every 12 in. along the front and back for added support. Once the cabinet is installed, cover the blocks with ¾-in. plywood, attached with 2-in. finish nails.

Euro levelers with applied kick panel. Commercially available cabinet levelers make supporting and leveling a cabinet a breeze. They attach to the bottom of the cabinet with a couple of screws and leave plenty of room for plumbing or ductwork. After installation, an applied kick panel is attached with proprietary clips that hold things in place and make future removal a snap, in case you ever have to access what's behind the kick. Follow the manufacturer's spacing and placement recommendations for best results.

A Euro-style cabinet leveler allows adjustment without the need for shims during installation.

Building wall cabinets

When you walk into a kitchen, the first thing you'll see is the wall cabinets. Set at eye level, they often completely cover the kitchen walls. When outfitted with glass doors or left without, they provide a great display area.

Wall cabinets offer opportunities for creative design. You can construct them from a different species from that used for the base cabinets, providing contrast. Or you can paint the wall cabinets but leave the base units natural. Or you can outfit the wall cabinets with a different style of door than that used on the base cabinets. So even though wall cabinets are half the size of base cabinets, they're just as, or even more, important to the overall kitchen design than the base units.

In this chapter, we'll examine building wall cabinets, including a couple of options for depth and strength. You'll learn a simple yet effective way to include adjustable shelving in cabinetry. Plus we'll cover a few ways to make shelves that can handle any load.

This wall cabinet uses species of contrasting colors. The frames are cherry, which provides a rich dark color, and the panels are lighter-toned maple. The pin holes on the interior allow the shelf height to be adjusted to suit the cabinets's contents.

Dimensioning wall cabinets

The construction of wall, or upper, cabinets, is much the same as for base cabinets. The main difference is the top of the cabinet. Instead of incorporating stretchers for attaching the countertop, wall cabinets have a fully enclosed top.

The standard depth of wall cabinets is 12 in. If you're building with plywood, you're faced with the same dilemma as when you build the base cabinets. A 48-in.-wide plywood sheet won't yield four sections of the required width because of the waste for saw kerfs. This time you're dealing with three kerfs of approximately ⅛ in. I usually adjust the cabinet depth to 11¾ in. when working with plywood. But sometimes, I cut three 12-in. side sections and use the remainder for shelves, which are slightly shallower. Or you can use any of the methods

Sizing the depth of the cabinet sides to 11¾ in. allows you to get four sides from standard-width plywood. With Melamine you can get the full 12-in. depth because the sheet is oversize.

The most common height for wall cabinet boxes is 30 in., but you can make boxes higher or shorter to suit your design. Just don't make them so tall that it's difficult to access the cabinet contents or the cabinets impinge on the work area below.

This wall cabinet features open shelving. The lower shelf has been reinforced with a solid-wood edgeband to reduce sag.

workSmart

When making notes on workpieces, use yellow chalk on wood or plywood and pencil on Melamine. The soft chalk won't mar the wood surface, and both chalk and pencil wipe right off with a little denatured alcohol.

discussed in Chapter 3 on base cabinets for achieving standard depth.

While there's no standard height for wall cabinets, 30 in. is common. Cabinets placed above appliances, such as refrigerators, will be much shorter, of course. And varying the heights of the cabinets in your kitchen can provide visual interest, like looking over a city skyline and seeing buildings of different heights.

I generally like to keep wall cabinets less than 3 ft. wide because of deflection. As you load a cabinet, the weight of the contents will cause the bottom of the cabinet (or a shelf) to deflect, or sag. As a general rule, for any given weight, the longer the span of a shelf or cabinet bottom, the greater the degree of deflection.

With base cabinets, the design decision is usually as simple as whether to include doors, drawers, or both. With wall cabinets the question is more about the doors—solid, glass-paned, or none at all. Wall cabinets with full doors are the most common type. But you can have a cabinet that's completely open with adjustable shelves to display items. Or you can combine doors and open space, for storage or display, into the same cabinet for even more versatility.

Begin sizing the box components by cutting sides to height, usually 30 in.

Building wall cabinet boxes

Wall cabinets, like base cabinets, are just simple boxes and are built in the same way (see Chapter 2). There are some variations that are specific to wall cabinets. For example, you can skip cutting the top stretchers and instead cut two "bottoms," one of which will serve as the top.

Remember to follow the basic cabinet strategy when cutting the parts to size. Side panels will vary in height. The depth can vary a bit as well, depending on the materials or techniques used, but will usually be between 11¾ in. and 12 in. deep. The bottom and the top will be the same depth as the sides. The nailers and top and bottom panels are sized roughly 1½ in. less than the cabinet's overall width. The exact amount will be twice the thickness of the sheet goods you're using for the cabinet. Be sure to measure the thickness of your materials, so that the finished size of your cabinet is what you planned.

The cutting sequence is the same as for the basic cabinet: Cut the sides to height; cut the sides, top, and bottom to depth; cut the top, bottom, and nailers to length; and finally cut the nailers to width. Once the parts are cut, groove for the back, if you're using an enclosed panel back. If you're installing an applied back, skip the groove (see "Reinforcing the back," p. 48).

A wall cabinet is enclosed at the top, so when you cut the bottom, cut two pieces of the same size. One will serve as the top.

Reinforcing the back

Base cabinets are held against the wall, but almost all of their support is directed straight down through the toekick assembly to the floor. This gives base cabinets a strong foundation and puts less stress on the rear nailers or back. Wall cabinets, on the other hand, are completely supported by the limited number of screws that pass through the nailers into the wall studs. The holding strength of wall cabinets depends on the strength of the nailer strip, the wall stud, and the screws used to hang the cabinet.

If you plan to store heavy items in your wall cabinets, consider using an applied back for added strength. An applied back can be made of the same ¾-in.-thick material as the cabinet walls, bottom, and top. The applied back replaces the much thinner ¼-in. back and the nailers behind it. Much more substantial than a narrow nailer, the continuous ¾-in. back helps spread the stresses of the hanging cabinet more evenly.

An applied back requires that you adjust your cutting and assembly strategy. When cutting components, reduce the depth of the sides, top, and bottom by roughly ¾ in. to accommodate the applied back. Be sure to measure carefully here because sheet goods vary in thickness, depending on type and origin. Eliminate the nailer strips

warning

Use strong steel screws for installing your wall cabinets. Avoid drywall screws for this application; they don't have the tensile or sheer strength of a true cabinet installation screw.

and the ¼-in. back from your cut list because the applied back takes the place of these components.

Shelving

Almost every upper cabinet I build contains adjustable shelves. They are an economical way to provide customizable storage solutions, depending on the homeowner's lifestyle. Your base cabinets can benefit from shelf pins as well. Adjustable shelves in base cabinets offer a lot of versatility and storage solutions with a minimum of work and expense, as compared to drawers or pullouts. And you can always upgrade your base cabinets later on, replacing the adjustable shelves with fancier pullouts, when it's convenient for you.

Usually, I make one or two shelves for each wall unit, but you can have as many shelves as make sense for the height of the cabinet. Removable ¼-in. shelf pins are an easy and quick way to provide shelf support.

For relatively narrow cabinets and light loads, a piece of ¾-in. edgebanded plywood provides an adequately strong shelf.

Shelf pins are a good way to support adjustable shelves. A shop-made or commercial template sets the distance of the holes from the edge and the holes from one another.

Lipped solid-wood banding on plywood is an effective way to reinforce a simple shelf. It is quick to make and strong enough for most household loads.

Types of shelves

Shelves can range from a simple slab of solid wood to a torsion box design, capable of supporting many times its own weight before showing signs of sag or deflection. Deflection is a function of the shelf's length, thickness, construction, material, and load. All of these factors together will determine whether your shelves stay straight and strong or bow in the middle.

Each type of shelf has pros and cons. Some shelves are heavy and complex but can hold a lot of weight. Other shelves are a cinch to make but deflect under modest loads. The simplest shelf consists of a piece of plywood or Melamine with an edgeband on the visible edge. This type of shelf would be perfect for a display cabinet holding only a few decorative plates or mugs. While an edgebanded plywood shelf is fine for light loads, it will deflect across a moderate span under minimal load.

A stronger shelf, adequate for most household loads, combines a piece of ¾-in. plywood glued to a rabbeted solid-wood edge. This type of shelf is strong and relatively easy to build. A lipped banded shelf should withstand most loads. Here are some types of the shelves I've used in the kitchens I have built.

Edgebanded plywood A piece of plywood with edgebanding applied to the visible edge is about as simple as it gets. This type of shelf is very quick to make, but not the strongest.

Solid-wood-banded plywood By adding a strip of solid hardwood, such as oak or hard maple, to the front of a plywood slab, you can reduce sag by about 25 percent. Simply glue the solid wood to the front edge of the shelf and trim it flush on both faces. If you're looking to increase strength without adding any perceived thickness to a shelf, this is a great way to go.

Lipped solid-wood banding on plywood This type of shelf is my standard for strength. I've built shelves, loaded with books, that span 3 ft. more, with no perceived sag. The only downside is this shelf looks thick or chunky, which may not look right in a contemporary design.

Solid hardwood A ¾-in. solid hardwood, such as maple or oak, has incredible strength and will resist sag significantly over plywood of the same thickness. This allows you to use a thinner shelf to support the same amount of weight.

Drilling holes for an adjustable shelf

I use a simple shopmade jig, combined with a plunge router and ¼-in. bit, to ensure evenly spaced holes. Before drilling, do a trial assembly and mark each side with an arrow pointing to the top. This will help reference the template during use.

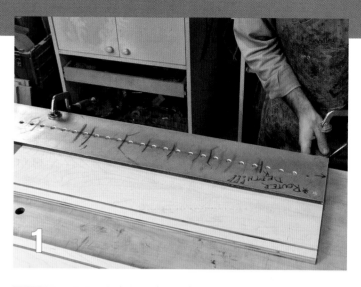

1. **Align the template with the top** and front or rear edge of the cabinet side, and secure the pieces with clamps. Aligning the template against the same edge ensures the holes will be aligned and the shelves level.

2. **Install a ⅜-in. guide bushing** and a ¼-in. spiral bit in your plunge router. With the bushing in one of the template's holes, plunge until the bit just touches the surface. Zero the bit depth mechanism on the router, and set the depth adjustment for a ½-in.-deep hole.

3. **Plunge the router to make holes** along the length of the template. Vacuum or blow off the dust, and inspect to make sure none of the holes were missed during the routing process. Reposition the template on the opposite edge of the cabinet side, reclamp, and repeat step 2. Then repeat the entire process on the other cabinet side, always aligning the jig with the top of the side.

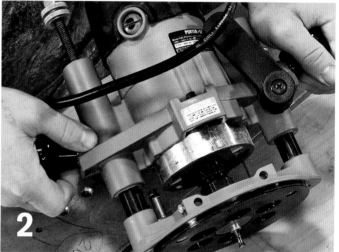

workSmart

If the length of the cabinet side exceeds the length of the template, you can extend the range of the jig by lining up one of the ¼-in. reference holes on the template with one of the holes drilled in the cabinet side.

Shelf-pin drilling jigs

A router makes a great tool for drilling shelf-pin holes, acting like a portable mini-drill press. Because I make cabinets professionally, my shelf-pin drilling jig is made from aluminum bar stock, but you can use ½-in. plywood. Size the plywood to be as long or longer than your cabinet side and about 5 in. wide. Draw a layout line centered on the plywood blank, along its entire length. Beginning at approximately 6 in. from the top edge, mark the centerline every 1¼ in. With a fence clamped to the drill press table to set a consistent distance, use a ¼-in. drill bit to drill a hole at each end of the jig for alignment. Chuck a ⅜-in. bit in the drill press and drill the remaining holes. Draw an arrow with permanent marker to indicate the top of the jig.

If you don't have a plunge router, you can use a commercial shelf-pin drilling jig and self-centering drill bit (usually available from the same source as the jig). Another option is to use a piece of pegboard as a guide and a standard drill bit with a stop collar to indicate when the drilling depth is achieved. If you use a handheld drill, be sure to keep it straight when drilling.

A drilling jig and self-centering bit will drill accurate holes.

SHELF PIN JIG

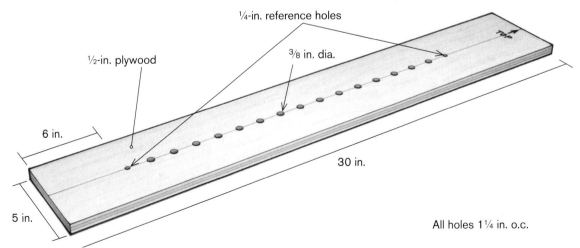

¼-in. reference holes

⅜ in. dia.

½-in. plywood

6 in.

30 in.

5 in.

All holes 1¼ in. o.c.

Reinforcing a shelf

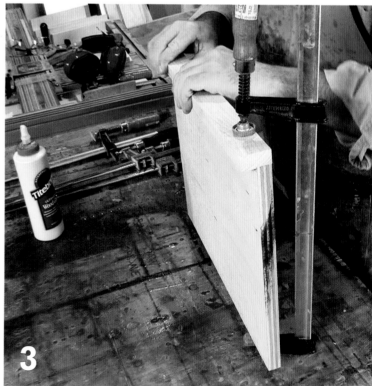

Most household shelving loads can be handled by the support of a piece of plywood edged in solid wood. This type of shelf is both strong and relatively easy to make. The solid-wood edging is rabbeted to aid in its placement and assembly, and then it's simply glued to the shelf. The lipped banding acts like a little I-beam, stiffening the shelf tremendously. Cut your shelf 1 in. shorter than the interior depth of the cabinet and ⅛ in. shorter than the interior width of the cabinet.

1. **Cut a piece of ¾-in. by 1½-in. hardwood** to the same length as the shelf slab. The species of the hardwood chosen should match the other woods used for the cabinet doors, face frames, or boxes.

2. **Set the rip fence of the tablesaw** to 1¹⁄₁₆ in. and raise the blade just a hair higher than the thickness of the shelf material. Run the solid banding through the saw on edge to cut a shallow rabbet.

3. **Glue the banding to the shelf** using yellow glue, then clamp it. Allow the assembly to dry overnight before removing the clamps. Then remove the excess glue with a card scraper.

4. **Trim the solid-wood banding flush** with the shelf using a handplane, trim router, or card scraper or by sanding. Be careful not to sand or cut into the plywood veneer.

5. **Ease the shelf and banding** with 150-grit sandpaper to remove any sharp edges. Then double-check the fit of the shelf in the cabinet. Make any necessary adjustments.

Building
face frames

Adding face frames to your cabinets gives your kitchen project a more traditional look. Face frames add a distinct border to the boxes, doors, and drawers, conveying the feeling that these are more than just boxes. Cabinets with face frames resemble built-in furniture.

Traditional cabinetry relied heavily on a face frame for structure and durability. The face frame was a critical component, providing strength for the storage area behind it as well as supporting drawers, slides, hinges, and other hardware. With the modular cabinets we're building, face frames act as a decorative element, although they do add some strength and rigidity to the cabinet box.

In this chapter, you'll learn how to build face frames quickly, using a modern method of joinery for this traditional component. You'll also learn how to connect them to the cabinet boxes. I'll discuss the modifications you'll need to make to the boxes to accommodate face frames as well as a quick technique for dressing them up.

Face frames give cabinets a classic look that suggests they are more than just simple storage boxes. Face-frame cabinetry is particularly appropriate in traditional-style homes.

Designing face-frame cabinets

In frameless, or Euro-style, cabinetry, you plan the width of the cabinet for a particular spot in the kitchen. You measure carefully and then build the box to that size. With face-frame cabinetry, the frame assembly is actually wider than the cabinet behind it, so first you make the face frame to the desired width and then build the cabinet slightly narrower.

Face frames, as well as the frames of doors and finish panels, are made up of two components: Vertical members, called stiles, and horizontal members, called rails. While there's no set rule that states what width the stiles and rails should be, I've found that a width of 2 in. achieves a well-proportioned, consistent look.

The demonstration that follows shows how to build face frames for one cabinet. Where two adjacent cabinets meet, designing stiles of half the normal width allows you to maintain the same spacing across a bank of cabinets. Although this creates a pleasing, uniform look, you might prefer to double up full-width stiles.

All face-frame stock is an equal width, so you can rip stiles and rails at the same time. A well-proportioned width for most cabinet projects is 2 in.

Don't rely on your skill with a measuring tape for consistent length pieces. Measure once and use a stop block to ensure all parts are the same length.

What to do if you don't own a planer

If you don't own a planer, check with your lumber supplier to see if they offer planning to thickness as an additional service (usually at a minimal charge). Another option is to enroll in a night class at a local high school or community college. Before I had the full complement of woodworking machines, I would enroll in a woodworking course and use the school's machinery two or three nights a week for a very modest fee. As a bonus, there's always an experienced woodworker overseeing the course who can help out in a pinch.

Cutting face-frame parts

To ensure flat face frames, be sure to use stock that is exactly the same thickness. I plane all of my lumber to ¾ in. The easiest way to ensure consistency is running the stock through a thickness planer. Joint one edge of the stock using a jointer or a long handplane (a #7 or #8 bench plane) to ensure the stock is straight. Then rip the stock to width. I generally make my face-frame components 2 in. wide, which I find visually pleasing. Plane, joint, and rip enough stile and rail stock to build all of the frames you'll need for the project.

Next, cut the stiles and rails. For each box, you'll need at least two stiles (upright members) and two rails (horizontal members). Cut your stiles to length using a miter gauge on the tablesaw or a stand-alone miter saw. The stiles should be cut ¾ in. longer than the height of the cabinet box. This provides a reveal to hide any imperfections in the cabinet box and adds an attractive detail.

Next cut the rails 4 in. shorter than the desired width of the face frame. You'll need one each for the top and bottom of the cabinet plus one for each drawer to act as a separator between it and a door or another drawer.

All pocket-hole jigs work on the same basic principle: a durable channel (in this case a hardened steel bushing) guides the drill bit as it cuts at a steep angle. Note the two-part step drill bit, especially designed for pocket holes.

Small portable pocket-hole jigs are inexpensive and useful for drilling cabinet sides to attach face frames.

Frame joinery

To join the rails and stiles, pocket screws provide a quick and secure connection. Even in multimillion-dollar homes, the pocket screw has become the standard for face-frame joinery.

You can use a drill press, Forstner bit, and shopmade angled auxiliary tables to drill pocket holes, but commercial jigs are affordable and easy to use. All of the commercial jigs work on the same principle—they provide a durable guide for the bit to drill a hole at a steep angle. End grain doesn't have the holding power of long grain, but driving the screw at an angle increases its purchase. The special two-step bit used to drill the holes has a smaller diameter pilot bit at the tip to drill the hole for the threaded part of the screw and a larger diameter auger-style bit to drill a larger hole to accommodate the screw head. The screws themselves have a pan head to seat securely at the bottom of the larger diameter hole.

Drill pocket holes in the rails in line with that piece's grain. Pocket holes placed across a stile create a weak point in the stile.

When assembling the joint, it's important to use the proper length fastener for the application and to keep

Always drill pocket holes in line with the grain. If you drill the holes cross grain (in the stiles), the joint will be weak.

workSmart

People often confuse which part of a frame is a rail and which part is a stile. One goes up and down and the other across. The way I remember is by thinking about a hand rail on a deck or stairway. The part I put my hand on is the rail, which is in a horizontal orientation. Therefore, the other component must be the stile.

The depth of the pocket hole is set by the position of the stop collar. In this jig, it's easily determined by laying the bit in the measuring scale.

Pan-head screws are meant to seat securely at the bottom of the pocket hole. Make sure to use the correct length screws for the job. For ¾-in. material, use 1¼-in. screws.

Angled plugs specially designed for concealing pocket holes are available in many common species.

the faces of the frame in the same plane. Clamping the frame assembly to your workbench is one way to ensure success. I prefer quick-adjusting clamps, made specifically for pocket screw joinery. Once the face frame is secured to the cabinet box, the pocket screw holes won't be noticeable, but if you want to conceal them, there are special angled plugs available to fill the hole.

Alternate methods of joining face frames

If you don't want to use pocket screws, there are alternatives. Here are a few of the joinery methods for building the face frame that I've used in kitchen projects.

Butt joints are the easiest way to build a face frame. Align the pieces and reinforce the joint with screws from the outside of the stiles. Drill and countersink for 3-in. screws in line with any rail assembly. To conceal the joint, you can plug the screw hole with a wooden plug, and flush trim it.

Lap joints are a very strong option for building face frames. Half-laps can be cut at the tablesaw, router table, or even with hand tools, but they require precise setup to ensure that frame components align in the same plane.

Biscuit joints are a quick, easy way to join frame members, but the standard biscuit jointer and biscuits are too wide for face frames. Special face-frame biscuits and cutters are available for some plate joiners, but they are far more expensive than a pocket screw jig set.

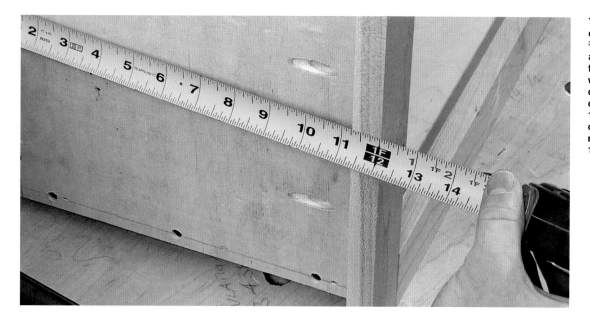

You build your cabinet boxes ¾ in. shallower to accommodate the face frame. Here, we've reduced the depth of the wall cabinet box to 11¼ in. so that the overall depth remains the usual 12 in.

Dowel joints are an effective way to join face frames if you already own a doweling jig. Keep in mind that a high-quality doweling jig costs as much as a pocket-hole jig, but cutting and aligning dowel joints takes more time.

Mortise-and-tenon joints are the traditional way to make face frames. While incredibly strong, the joint is time-consuming to produce. Save it for your finest furniture.

Modifying cabinet boxes for face frames

Cabinets built for face frames are smaller than those for frameless cabinets. You'll reduce the depth of your cabinet sides by the thickness of the face frame, usually ¾ in. The cabinet box will be narrower than the overall width of the frame itself. I usually build cabinets with an overall width that is 2 in. narrower than the frame's overall width.

Unlike frameless cabinets, cabinets intended for face frames do not need to be edge-banded because the face frame covers the exposed edges of the plywood or Melamine. Nor do you need to add a stretcher to separate a drawer or door in the cabinet. Instead, you'll add additional rails to the face frames.

Cabinet and face-frame math

If you adjust the dimensions of the frame's stiles, for example, where two cabinets meet, you'll also need to adjust the size of the cabinet width accordingly. The cabinet's overall width should be 2 in. wider than the distance between the stiles. Here's how the math works out: To keep a ¼-in. reveal from the inside edge of the face frame to the inside of the cabinet box, just double the reveal to arrive at ½ in. Now add the thickness of the two sides to this measurement. Two sides of ¾-in. material yields approximately 1½ in. Now add ½ in. for the reveal. The result is 2 in. Since material thickness varies, make sure your face frames are made precisely to the width needed for the run of cabinets you've planned. Adjust your cabinet width based on the exact thickness of the material or use a slightly larger offset and stick with the 2-in. rule of thumb.

Joining frames with pocket screws

Drill two holes per rail for optimal strength and to keep the rails from twisting before the assembly is secured to the cabinet box. Your jig may differ from the one shown here. Be sure to familiarize yourself with your jig's operation by cutting some test pieces.

1. **Begin by laying out the pieces** and marking them with chalk so that you know which part goes where.

2. **Position the frame member in the jig** so you are drilling into the correct side (in this jig, so it faces you). Line it up to the marks in the jig and secure it with the clamp.

3. **Drill until the stop collar reaches the top of the guide bushing.** You may need to raise the bit to clear shavings before you reach the bottom of the hole. Repeat for the second hole.

4. **Secure the joint with the pocket-hole clamp.** Make sure to align the frame members precisely.

5. **Drive the screws** with the square-drive pocket-screw driver until the head seats at the bottom of the pocket hole.

6. **Work your way around the frame,** aligning the frame members, clamping, and driving screws.

7. **The finished frame** is square and strong.

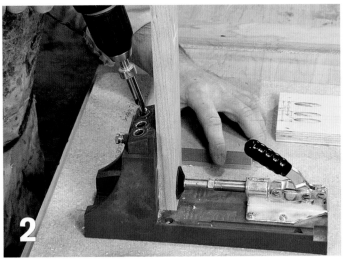

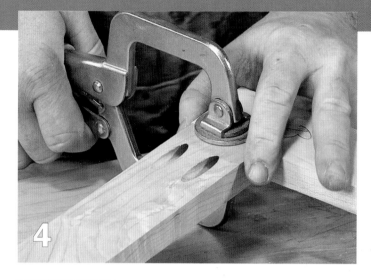

workSmart

Don't measure when adding the drawer separator because you could be off a hair from side to side. Instead, use a spacer block to ensure consistent location of rails.

Attaching face frames
to cabinets

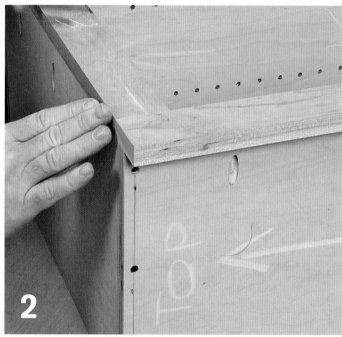

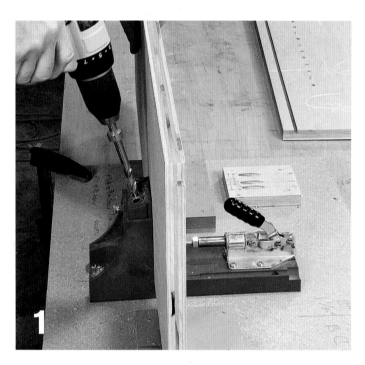

W hile you could glue and nail the face frame to the cabinet, you'll need to fill the nail holes afterward. The putty never quite matches the finish, and you'll have to clean up the glue squeeze-out. Biscuits would also work but are fussy to align. A strong and efficient way to secure the face frame is to use pocket screws.

1. **Drill a series of pocket holes** along the front edge of the outside face of the cabinet sides, bottom, and top or top nailer. Space the holes 6 in. to 8 in. apart.

2. **Align the face frame** with the top edge of the cabinet, centered along the cabinet's width.

3. **Check the reveal** on the inside of the cabinet. It should be ¼ in. from the cabinet side to the inside of the frame.

4. **Clamp the face frame to the cabinet.** The proprietary clamps shown here hold the face frame to the cabinet while you attach it, but any long clamp that will reach from the front of the frame to the back of the cabinet will work too.

5. **Drive the pocket screws,** starting at the top and working your way down to the bottom of the case. Install the pocket screws evenly on both sides as you work. Check your reveals as you go, making sure they're even, which will ensure that the cabinet is square to the frame.

workSmart

The easiest way to drill the pocket holes is to cut them before you assemble the cabinets. If you forget, you can drill the pocket holes after assembly. A small portable pocket screw jig is particularly handy for this purpose. The process is the same and works nearly as well as drilling before assembly, but it takes longer.

Although proprietary pocket-hole clamps are quick and efficient, you can also hold the face frame in position by clamping it to your workbench or assembly table.

Adding a bead

A simple applied bead can add a high-end decorative touch to your face frames. It's simple to make the bead stock with a router table outfitted with a ¼-in. beading bit. Begin with ¾-in. stock ripped into ¾-in.-wide strips. You'll get two strips of beading from each blank, so cut enough blanks to cover the inside perimeter of all the cabinet openings.

1. **Install a ¼-in. beading bit** into a table-mounted router. Adjust the bit height so the bottom edge of the bead is even with the router table, and adjust the router fence so it is even with the inside edge of the bead's radius.

2. **Rout a bead on one edge** of the blank. Flip the blank and cut another bead.

3. **Set the tablesaw rip fence** to a distance of ¼ in. Rip the bead from each side of the blank.

4. **Miter each end of the bead** to fit into the cabinet opening. It is critical that your cut is precisely 45 degrees to ensure miter joints without gaps.

5. **Attach the bead** flush to the back edge of the face frame with a thin line of glue. Use a small pin nailer to hold the bead in place while the glue dries; you can also clamp it.

6. **The finished bead.**

warning

When working with thin stock, use a push stick to keep your fingers away from spinning bits and rotating sawblades.

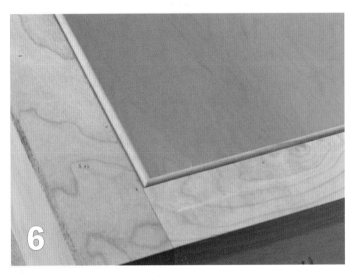

Building drawer boxes

Drawers and pullouts increase the efficiency of cabinets. No one likes to search for something in the back of a cabinet while in the middle of cooking dinner. Drawers and pullouts that travel effortlessly on modern drawer slides bring their contents to you, within easy reach.

The difference between a drawer and a pullout is mostly semantics. Both are boxes with a mechanism allowing them to open and close easily. Generally, if a drawer is placed behind a door, it's called a pullout. If it has its own face on the front of the cabinet, it's called a drawer.

Drawers take a lot of stress from opening and closing, especially on the drawer front. Joints that direct stress away from the front make the drawer more durable.

There are countless joinery options for creating drawers, but we'll focus on two types of joinery. The first, assembled with pocket screws, is quick to build and assemble. The second type is a classic dovetailed drawer that's also quick to build once you properly set up a router and jig.

A pullout is nothing more than a drawer that hides behind a door. It is particularly handy for storing pots and pans and pantry goods. If a pullout will bear heavy loads, plan on using heavy-duty drawer slides and thicker (½ in.) plywood for the bottom.

Designing drawer boxes

The dimensions of the drawer boxes depend on several factors besides the dimensions of the cabinet. Before you begin construction of any drawer, choose your hardware and joinery method and the style of your drawer front. If you've built face-frame cabinetry, make certain you understand the implications for the width of the drawer boxes. Here are some considerations to keep in mind.

Hardware

Commercial drawer slides have clearances that must be incorporated into the design of the drawer and, in some cases, the cabinet itself. So it's best to have the hardware and technical specifications in hand before you start to design your drawers. You'll also have to decide whether your drawers will have the slides mounted on the sides or bottom because this choice can affect the dimensions of the drawer box.

Determining the height of a dovetailed drawer

After you've set up your router and half-blind dovetail jig, make sample joints at different heights. This will help you determine the optimal height that will yield even pin and tail spacing. The spacing can then be varied, usually in 1-in. increments. My jig provides even spacing at $^{15}/_{16}$ in. The drawers I make are in 1-in. increments after that: $2^{15}/_{16}$ in., $3^{15}/_{16}$ in., $4^{15}/_{16}$ in., and so on.

To install drawer hardware in face-frame cabinets, you'll need to add strips of plywood or other material to bring it high enough to clear the frame.

Joinery

If you're building a simple drawer box with butt joints reinforced with pocket screws, you have more latitude with drawer heights. Half-blind dovetails cut on a universal jig such as the one we show here have tails and pins of a fixed width. A very thin pin at the end can crack during assembly or fail under stress, so plan your drawer heights so that you end up with approximately a half pin at the ends.

Cabinet modifications

Face-frame cabinets will require some modification to accommodate the drawer slides. You'll need to provide a means of bringing the slider away from the cabinet side so that it can clear the frame (this is covered in Chapter 8). Choose your drawer slides before you start building and understand how to install them in the cabinets before determining the dimensions of the drawers.

Drawer fronts

The drawer fronts and doors are the public face of your cabinets. They create the overall style of the cabinetry, whether traditional or modern.

Overlay vs. inset drawers Overlay drawers, as the name suggests, overlay the cabinet box and stretchers or the face frame. Full-overlay drawers are completely outside the frame or cabinet box. Lipped or partial-overlay drawers have part of the drawer front inside the frame or cabinet and a lip that overlays the cabinet face. The advantage of overlay drawers is their ability to hide any gaps or imperfections in the cabinet opening. They are also much less fussy to install. You don't need to pay as much attention to tolerances when fitting them, and they provide their own built-in mechanical stop. Inset or flush drawers have a clean, refined look but require careful fitting to ensure that the gap around the drawer front is consistent.

Applied front vs. integral front Most of the drawers I build have an applied front, which means I build the drawer box and add a covering of solid wood or a panel to complete the drawer. Applied fronts have many advantages. You can build your boxes without worrying about the exact dimensions of the front, so drawer production is faster. You can also use the same material for all sides of the drawer box, which is handy when you're cutting

The cabinet on the left has inset drawers and doors that are flush with the face frame. The cabinet on the right has full-overlay drawers and doors. The side panel covers the door and drawer edges and any joinery (such as pocket screws on the outside face of the cabinet side).

drawer parts. An applied front will work for either overlay or inset drawers. For inset drawers, the final adjustment of an applied front is much easier to finesse than for an integral front.

On the other hand, an integral front, joined to the drawer box with half-blind dovetails, is considered a mark of craftsmanship. You can still cut the dovetails with a router jig, but the setup takes more time. Integral fronts can also be joined to the box using pinned rabbets, sliding dovetails, or locking rabbet joints, among other options.

Proportion

If your cabinets have a top drawer over a door or a bank of drawers, it's best to make all the top drawers to the same height. If you're planning for drawers below, proportion them, don't just take the remaining space and divide it by the number of drawers. There are several mathematical ways to arrive at a pleasing proportion. For more on ways to proportion drawers, consult one of the design resources listed on p. 120.

An integral drawer front gives a finished appearance, but incorporating one takes careful planning and stock preparation to avoid gaps around the opening of the drawer.

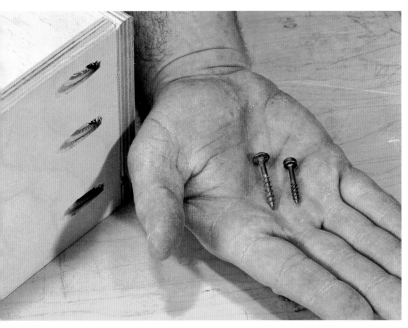

Be sure to use the right size pocket screws for the material. For ½-in.-thick material, you'll use 1-in. screws. Screws that are too long can come through on the opposite side, which may cause problems when you apply the front.

Once set up, a dovetail jig can quickly produce dovetailed drawers and pullouts. The keys are to use material of the same thickness, set the router bit to the correct height, and mark parts for reference.

Choosing joinery for drawers

A kitchen project often requires many drawers. So one of the key factors in deciding on a drawer building method is time. Pocket screws and router-cut half-blind dovetails are both relatively quick.

Pocket screw drawers

Building a drawer with pocket screws is simple and fast. It's a great way to build the drawers required for a whole roomful of cabinets.

The pocket screws pass through the front and back of the drawer box into the sides, acting like small tenons to keep the drawer together. They transfer the stress of opening and closing the drawer from the front to the sides. You won't see the pocket holes because the front of the drawer will be covered. If you choose, you can plug the holes on the back.

My material of choice for building drawers and pullouts is ½-in. Baltic birch plywood, which is sold in 5-ft. by 5-ft. sheets. Because it's imported from overseas, Baltic birch is manufactured to metric specifications. Its actual thickness is 12 mm, a hair thinner than ½ in.

Router-cut half-blind dovetails

Dovetails are very strong, offering a lot of glue surface and a mechanically locking corner. Plus they're one of the hallmarks of fine craftsmanship.

When I have a large number of dovetailed drawers to build for a kitchen, I turn to a common half-bind dovetail jig. Almost every woodworking store or catalog sells a version of this jig, and the one you get may be a bit different from mine, but the theory behind them all is the same. Even so, there are some tricks that speed the process.

There's no short cutting the setup on these jigs. Expect to spend some time getting it just right. But once the jig is dialed in, you can really crank out drawers. Keep in mind that any change to your router bit height or your stock thickness will change the quality of the joint you cut with one of these jigs.

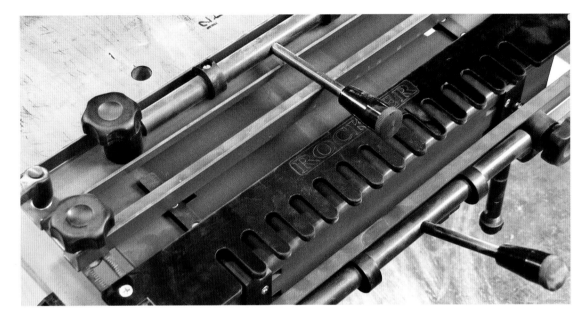

Universal dovetail jigs, such as the one shown here, are available from many suppliers. Although they all work on the same basic principle, each has its own technical specifications so read the setup instructions carefully and rout test pieces to make sure you've got it right.

Other Joinery Options

Every joint has pros and cons, from relative strength to ease to create and appearance. Here are some options:

Rabbet Quick and easy to make, this joint is almost as simple as a pocket screw drawer. A benefit of rabbet joints over pocket screws is there are no exposed fasteners. Over time, rabbet joints break down under the stress of opening and closing the drawer.

Pinned rabbet Pinning a standard rabbet joint with a few hardwood dowels helps bring strength to the joint. The pins do a good job of directing the stress of opening a drawer from its front to its sides.

Locking rabbet Also known as a rabbeted tongue-and-dado joint, this joint is a step above the standard rabbet joint. A locking rabbet provides a mechanical connection that strengthens the joint. This joint is fairly complex to set up, but once done, you can produce drawers quickly.

Box joints The multiple glue surfaces on the many interlocking fingers make this joint extremely strong. Box joints can also be a design element, especially when made with contrasting woods. Cutting this joint requires only a tablesaw and a simple shopmade jig but can take as much or more time than a half-blind dovetail with a jig.

Box, or finger, joints can be cut on a tablesaw with a simple shopmade jig. The many fingers create multiple long-grain to long-grain glue surfaces, which make the joint very strong.

Cutting parts for a pocket screw drawer

Just as when cutting cabinet case parts, consistency is key when cutting parts for drawers. Cut all the parts that share the same setting before adjusting your settings. You may wish to review the process for building a basic cabinet in Chapter 2 to see how to organize the cutting sequence and set up the saw to groove for the bottom.

1. **Rip the drawer blanks to height.**

2. **Crosscut the sides to the desired length.** The standard depth for base cabinet drawers is 22 in.

3. **Mark the parts** after you cut them so they can be easily identified for joinery and assembly.

4. **Crosscut the front and back** of the drawer to the desired width minus twice the drawer thickness. Remember to deduct clearances for your drawer slides, but be sure to check the specifications for your hardware installation.

5. **Cut the drawer bottom** from ¼-in. plywood. Size the bottom ½ in. wider than your drawer front and ½ in. shorter than the length of your drawer side.

6. **Cut ¼-in.-deep grooves** along the lower edge of each piece to hold the drawer bottom. Locate this groove about ½ in. from the bottom edge.

> **workSmart**
>
> If you're planning to store heavy items, such as pots and pans, in a drawer, consider upgrading to ½-in. plywood for the bottom. It's stronger than ¼-in. material and won't deflect as much under heavy loads.

Rounding drawer parts

To make drawers more user-friendly, I ease the top edges with a bullnose bit in the router table. You can do the same with a roundover or beading bit, or by breaking the sharp edges with sandpaper.

1. **Set up a ½-in.-dia. bullnose bit** in the router table, aligning the bottom of the radius with the table surface and the fence with the inside of the radius.

2. **Rout the top of the drawer,** holding it firmly against the fence, moving from right to left.

3. **The rounded top edge** gives a nice appearance and is friendly to the touch.

> **workSmart**
>
> You can also use a ½-in. roundover bit for this operation. In the router table, set up the bit so that the bottom of the radius is just below the table surface. Align the fence so that it is in the same plane with the bearing. Rout the radius on one side of the drawer part, then flip it over and rout the other. If you don't have a router table, you can use a handheld router. Just make sure to clamp your workpiece securely to the bench.

Building a pocket screw drawer

With most pocket-hole jigs, you'll need to adjust your drill depth and jig setup to accommodate the thinner drawer stock. But once that's out of the way, you can crank out drawer boxes in no time flat.

1. **Adjust the stop collar** on the step bit to the recommended position for the thickness of the material you're using to build your drawer boxes.

2. **Secure the drawer part** (front or back) in the jig with the side you will drill facing the bushings. (On this jig, the outside face of the drawer part faces you.)

3. **Drill pocket screw holes** in the ends of each drawer front and back. Generally, I space these holes every 2 in. to 3 in. o.c.

> **workSmart**
>
> Solid wood expands and contracts across its grain in response to seasonal humidity changes. When using solid wood for drawers, be sure to orient the grain horizontally, so seasonal wood movement won't stress the joints.

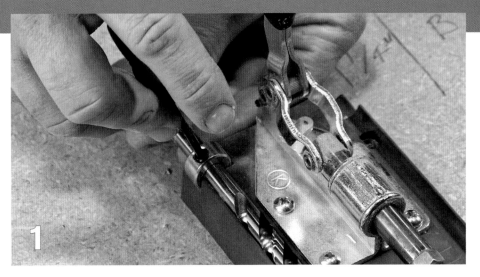

Building a pocket screw drawer (continued)

4. **Align the corner joints** of the front and sides and hold in place with clamps.

5. **Drive pocket screws** until seated to secure the joint.

6. **Install the bottom** and position the back. Clamp the back and drive pocket screws to complete the joinery.

7. **Check the drawer for square** by measuring across the diagonals, which should be exactly the same length. If necessary, loosen the screws, then clamp the drawer box into square and redrive the screws.

workSmart

You can also use standard bar clamps to hold the drawer parts in place during assembly.

Preparing parts for a dovetailed drawer

For best results, use components that are exactly the same thickness. If you're using plywood, buy all you'll need for the drawer boxes at the same time. If you're using solid wood for the drawer parts, plane it all at the same time to the same setting. Before cutting any drawer parts, familiarize yourself with your dovetail jig and the settings, so that you can size the parts correctly.

1. **Rip the drawer parts to height.**

2. **Crosscut the front and backs** to the desired width of the drawer, remembering to account for slide clearance. Crosscut the sides, which are cut about ½ in. shorter than the desired finished length of the drawer. This measurement may vary, depending on your dovetail jig. Be sure to check before cutting parts.

3. **Mark all components for reference,** indicating whether the part is a side or a front/back.

4. **Assign each drawer a number** and write it on the top edge of each piece to keep parts organized. This system also makes it easier to orient the drawer parts in the jig.

Cutting half-blind dovetails with a jig

This demonstration shows the process of cutting half-blind dovetails with my jig. Follow the instructions for your own jig carefully. Before cutting any drawer parts, you'll need to set up and adjust your router and the jig. *Don't skip this step!*

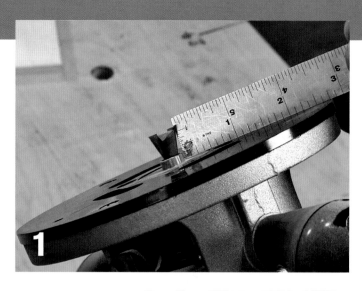

1. **Set up your router** so that the bit is at the height recommended by the jig manufacturer. Make test cuts in stock of the exact same thickness as your drawer parts until the joint fits properly.

2. **Insert a drawer side in the vertical portion** of the jig, with the inside of the part facing out. This will be the tail board. Tails must always be on the drawer sides to take maximum advantage of the mechanical strength of the pin locking into the dovetail socket.

3. **Place the pin board in the horizontal portion** of the jig. The inside will face up. Always be sure the reference numbers are facing the outside of the jig. Note that the workpieces rest against stops that determine their relative position in the jig.

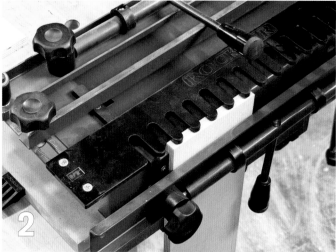

workSmart

Setting up a half-blind dovetail jig takes a lot of time to get it just right. One way I speed up the process is to make a template for setting the router bit height. Once I have the jig set up, I rout through the end of a notched board. That way if I ever have to change the router bit, returning to the proper setup is as simple as lining up the bit to the routed recess in the board.

4. **Make a scoring cut to reduce tearout.**

5. **Rout along the template fingers.** *Never lift the router, or you'll ruin the joint.* Try to hold the router at the same angle while making the cuts. Turning it could magnify any irregular offset from the guide bushing.

6. **Rotate the pieces** so the uncut sides are positioned for cutting. Make sure the reference numbers are facing out. Repeat the scoring and template cuts.

7. **Test-fit the drawer.** During this dry-fit, take a measurement for the drawer bottom panel, which will be ½ in. wider and ½ in. longer than the interior of the drawer. Cut the drawer bottom from a piece of ¼-in. plywood.

workSmart

Dovetail bits get hot fast and are prone to breakage due to their small diameter at the shank. Letting the bit cool for 5 or 10 minutes between drawers will extend its life considerably. I always keep a spare bit on hand, just in case of a failure. But bits are not always interchangeable. I always make test joints whenever I have to change bits or any aspect of my setup.

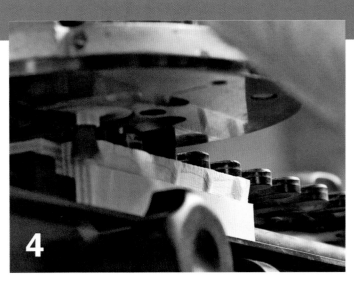

Assembling a dovetailed drawer

A well-executed dovetail holds itself together without the need for clamping pressure. Test-fit the joinery before applying glue. You may wish to round over the top of the drawer side as shown on p. 74.

1. **Rout the groove for the drawer bottom** with a ¼-in. dado blade, set a hair higher than ¼ in. Line up the center of the bottom socket with the blade. By cutting the groove so that it will end in a socket, you'll hide the cut.

2. **Begin with a tail board** (the board with the sockets) on the bench and the mating pin boards off to each side. Put a drop of yellow glue on the sides of each socket.

3. **Press the pin board onto the tails** and seat the joint. Repeat with the opposite pin board.

4. **Slide the bottom into place** and squeeze a dab of glue into the open sockets.

5. **Position the remaining tail board** into the sockets and tap the joint home. Inspect all the joints to ensure they're seated.

6. **Check the drawer for square** by measuring the diagonals. Make any adjustments to bring it into square. When everything looks good, set the drawer aside to dry. After an hour or so, you can come back and peel away any squeeze-out.

Dealing with glue squeeze-out

When you're ready to assemble your dovetailed drawer, go easy with the glue. Just a little dab in each side of the socket does the trick. Too much glue means you'll have to deal with excess glue squeeze-out later.

To avoid the need to scrape much glue, you can apply painter's tape to the inside of the joint during your dry-fit stage. Any squeeze-out will run on to the tape and peel off with the tape once removed.

You can also prefinish the drawer interiors. Most white and yellow glues don't bond well to finished surfaces, which makes peeling dried squeeze-out a breeze. I apply one coat of finish to the inside faces of the drawer after I cut the components to size but before cutting the dovetail joints, and let the finish dry overnight. (For more on finishing, see Chapter 9.)

Doors, drawer fronts, and panels

It's time to dress up the boxes by adding doors, drawer fronts, and finish panels. There are many styles to choose from, although some require more skill and tooling to make. In this chapter, I'm going to show you how to build a frame using a mortise-and-tenon joint. Once you've mastered the basic technique, you'll be able to make a variety of frame-and-panel assemblies for doors, drawer fronts, and panels. The difference between these is mostly size. Finish panels, which cover the exposed edges of the cabinets, are just doors fastened to a cabinet side. Drawer fronts are like small doors, but rather than being hinged to the cabinet, they're fastened to a drawer box.

I'll show you how to build several types of doors, drawer fronts, and panels. One of my favorites is a Shaker-style frame-and-panel assembly that's very adaptable. This style looks equally at home in both traditional and contemporary settings. I'll also show you how to size doors, drawer fronts, and panels and a couple of tricks to make it easier to scribe and fit these elements.

The clean lines of the Shaker-style doors, drawer front, and finish panel on this cabinet allow it to be at home in both traditional and contemporary settings. The door and drawer front are inset in a matching face frame, but this type of panel could also be used for overlay doors and drawers.

Design considerations

Before you begin building doors or drawers, choose the hardware for opening and closing them. As discussed in Chapter 6, choose the drawer slides before you make the drawer boxes. You'll also need to pick the door hinges because your choice could affect the dimensions of the doors or the cabinet boxes. Finish panels, of course, are a simpler part of the project, unaffected by hardware choices. The only hardware needed for finish panels is screws to attach them to the cabinet.

In the case of doors and drawers, you must also choose whether they will be overlay or inset. Overlay doors and drawers are easier to fit, but inset styles have a more refined look. You may wish to review the discussion of inset vs. overlay drawers on p. 68 to see how the differences will affect your design. Remember that if you're building face-frame cabinets, you'll need to build up the inside of the cabinet wall to install the hardware.

One way to dress up panels is to add stock molding. In this case, it's glued and tacked to the panel, giving the door a traditional look. You can also apply moldings to slab panels.

One of the simplest types of doors is the board-and-batten style. Horizontal battens attached to the back of the uprights keep the door flat.

A simple slab door works perfectly with sleek, contemporary designs. In this Euro-style cabinet, the full overlay door and drawer front and the finish panel are edgebanded plywood.

Style and construction options

When it comes to choosing the style of your doors, drawer fronts, and panels, there are many possibilities. They range from simple slabs of plywood to intricate coped and angled joinery. The skill, tooling, and time required to build them varies accordingly. Here are just a few examples of the options available to you

Slab The simplest of doors and panels is a slab of edgebanded plywood made to size. This style lends itself well to sleek contemporary settings.

Slab with applied molding This style offers the look of a raised panel without all the work. Common molding from the home center is applied to the face of a panel to transform it into something that looks traditional. Unless you can match the molding to the species of the panel or stain it to match closely, this technique is best reserved for projects that will be painted.

Board and batten A series of vertical boards held in place by horizontal members, the batten door lends itself well to rustic settings and primitive styles.

Frame and panel A framework of rails and stiles surrounds a panel for a classic furniture or cabinetry look. Details on the edges of the frames can be varied, and panels can range from simple flat plywood slabs to solid-wood raised arch tops and cathedral panels. In commercial cabinetry, frame-and-panel doors have become the standard.

Faux molded panel Like the slab door with applied molding, this is a quick way to achieve a traditional look without all the work. This works best when the doors will be painted.

Glass doors Generally a form of frame-and-panel door, glass doors can also be made in conjunction with plywood slabs. Solo glass doors special ordered from glass suppliers involve specialized hinges, advanced skills, and exacting measurements.

Single vs. multiple doors

There's no hard and fast rule on when to make more than one door for a cabinet. The decision is partially dictated by design, but it's also somewhat subjective. I start to think about two doors when the width of the cabinet reaches 18 in. to 24 in. As a general rule, I never make any single cabinet door wider than 24 in. In my opinion, this is just too wide for a single door and places more weight and stress on the hinges. More important, the additional weight stresses the joinery. Once you've made the decision to use two doors, the process of measuring the door opening and sizing the door, including room for gaps, remains the same. Just remember to add the gap between the doors to your measurements.

Slab vs. frame and panel for a drawer front

There's also no rule about when to switch drawer front styles, so rely on common sense and your eye for this decision. At some point, a frame-and-panel drawer front is so out of proportion, it looks absurd. On my cabinets, I use 7 in. as the minimum height or width for a frame-and-panel drawer front. Here's why.

Frame-and-panel drawer fronts are made the same as doors, with 2½-in. rails and stiles, so 5 in. of the drawer face will be covered with framework. You'll also need to factor in the size of the panel; if it's only ½ in. to 1 in., it will look completely out of proportion. I shoot for at least a 2-in. panel. That plus 5 in. of framework yields the 7-in. minimum size.

A solid drawer front looks better on drawers less than 7 in. in height or width. Larger drawers can be covered with a frame-and-panel drawer front.

For drawer spaces less than 7 in., I use slab fronts of the same species as the rest of the framework. Banded plywood works well, but solid wood can be used too. Just remember that solid wood is subject to seasonal expansion and contraction, so allow for it when figuring the dimensions of the drawer fronts.

Sizing panels

While the doors, finish panels, and drawer fronts of your cabinets all share the same construction techniques and style, figuring out what size they should be requires careful measurement and calculation. How well you do this will determine how much effort and time the final fitting will take. In the case of a door or drawer front, you'll want to make the panel a little smaller than the cabinet, or the opening in the face frame. In the case of a finish panel, you'll want to make it a little bigger, to allow for scribing and fitting during installation.

Build finish panels slightly oversize to allow for scribing to wall irregularities.

Doors and drawer fronts

A narrow gap around the perimeter of a door shows off your skill as a cabinetmaker, because achieving a narrow, consistent gap requires exacting measurement, a square door and cabinet, and perfect hinging. Some fine furniture makers build doors larger than the opening, or cabinet, then trim them down with handplanes, making them fit the openings exactly. Unless you're really confident using a handplane and you have the time for this exacting work, follow the guidelines below.

To start, aim for a gap of $\frac{1}{16}$ in. all around. The gap can always be made larger by trimming the door, but reducing the size of the gap afterward gets tricky. So start tight and increase the gap if necessary. Adjusting the gap will help conceal tiny errors if the cabinet opening or the panel you're fitting isn't square or sized exactly. If you finally end up with a $\frac{1}{8}$-in. gap, that's fine. It's more important that all the gaps are consistent. On inset doors and drawers, your eye will instantly see any inconsistencies.

Let's look at an example. I'm building a single door on an 18-in.-wide Euro-style wall cabinet. I plan to make the door $17\frac{7}{8}$ in. wide and $29\frac{7}{8}$ in. high. This will leave me with a tight $\frac{1}{16}$-in. gap all the way around. I've basically just measured the cabinet's overall dimensions and subtracted $\frac{1}{8}$ in. from the height and width. I follow these guidelines whether for an overlay door on a frameless cabinet or an inset door on a face frame. Where a door meets a drawer front or another door, just factor in another $\frac{1}{16}$ in. for the gap.

Finish panels

Finish panels are applied to the outside edges of cabinet boxes to cover the screws, staples, and raw plywood. Ultimately, they are the transition between the cabinet box and the wall of the home, so there should be no noticeable gaps. Most walls in a home are not perfectly straight due to variations in stud lumber and taping and finishing the drywall. For a tight fit, scribe the panel to the wall and cut it to match the wall's irregularities. Some of the panel's material will be removed, so begin with an oversize panel. I generally figure an extra $\frac{1}{4}$-in. depth for my finish panels, which is enough to allow adjustment for most walls.

To calculate the width of a finish panel for a face-frame cabinet, just measure the distance from the back of the cabinet to the back edge of the face frame. Then add the $\frac{1}{4}$ in. to allow for scribing. It's that simple.

Making a finish panel for a Euro-style cabinet with overlay doors is a bit different. Begin by measuring the overall depth of the cabinet and add ¼ in. for scribing. Next, add an additional ⅞ in. to the measurement to accommodate the thickness of the doors as well as a slight offset introduced by the hinges. There's no need to alter the height of a finish panel, so plan on making it the same height as your cabinet.

When you're finished building the panel, cut a ¼-in. rabbet ½ in. deep on the edge that will mate to the wall. This removes the bulk of the material from the edge and will make scribing a little easier. For more on scribing, consult one of the trim carpentry resources on p. 120.

Installing finish panels and drawer fronts

Applying a finish panel to a face-frame cabinet side is as simple as shimming out the panel, so it's flush with the face frame, and attaching it from the inside of the cabinet. Just drive a few screws through the box and into the framework of the panel.

Use screws that are long enough to hold the panel in place but short enough so they don't penetrate through the face. Once attached, you can adjust any unwanted reveals by planing or sanding the face frame flush to the finish panel.

In frameless applications, the job of attaching a finish panel is even easier, since there's nothing to shim and nothing to plane down later. Just make sure the leading edge of the finish panel is proud of the cabinet box by ⅞ in. so it lines up in the same plane as the doors. If you're applying a finish panel to an open-face cabinet that doesn't have doors, you can just bring the panel flush to the front edge.

When attaching drawer fronts, I position the panel in place and hold it there using hot glue, double-sided tape, or a brad or two fired from my pneumatic nailer. Then I attach the panel permanently using a few screws driven through the drawer box and into the framework of the panel. With a solid slab of wood, I use screws placed only halfway up its height so wood movement isn't restricted.

Position the finish panel, aligning it carefully, and clamp it to the cabinet side with spring clamps.

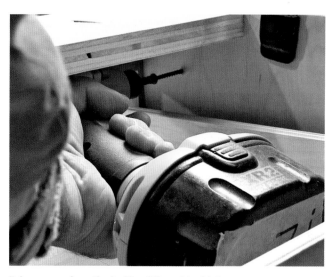

Drive screws from the inside of the cabinet into the frame of the side panel or directly into the panel if frameless. Make sure you use screws long enough to hold the panel but not so long that they will poke through the other side.

Building a slab panel or door

Nothing could be simpler than a slab of plywood with edgebanding. You could use iron-on banding tape, or in high-wear situations, like door fronts, doors, and corner panels, use solid wood edgebanding, which is somewhat more durable and allows slightly more room for adjustments. Make sure you account for the thickness of the strips when sizing the plywood, and rip enough material ⅛ in. to ³⁄₁₆ in. thick to cover the edges of all the panels you're making.

◖workSmart

Prefinishing the plywood panel makes it easier to manage glue squeeze-out. You can just wipe away the excess with a damp rag.

1. **Begin by gluing the strips** to the top and bottom of the panel. Use battens to ensure even clamping pressure.

2. **Trim the ends of the top and bottom strips,** if necessary, and remove any glue that might interfere with the contact of the side strips; then glue and clamp the strips as in the previous step.

3. **Remove any glue squeeze-out** while it's soft, scraping carefully to avoid damaging the plywood veneer. Trim the ends of the banding so it's flush to the sides, and ease the edges with a block plane or sandpaper.

Making a mortise-and-tenon frame

There are many ways to build a frame, but not all are created equal. Dowels are tricky to align. Rail and stile router bits require careful setup, and the resulting joint isn't that strong. The method shown here has the virtue of simplicity and strength. It can be cut entirely on the tablesaw with just a few setups. If you like, you can dress up the frame with beads and moldings for a more traditional look.

1. **Rip ¾-in.-thick frame stock** to 2½ in. wide. For a consistent width throughout your kitchen project, it's smart to rip as much frame stock as you'll need for all the panels you're building, whether door fronts, doors, or finish panels.

2. **Crosscut two stiles per panel** to the desired height of the frame.

Consistency is the key to square, flat frames

Just as for face frame or cabinet parts, consistency is essential to success. If you mill all of your frame parts to exactly the same thickness, the grooves and the tenons will line up. Any variation in thickness will mean that the groove may be centered on some frame members and offset on others. Variations are doubled in the tenons because you're cutting on both faces. For that reason, it pays to mill all your stock to the same setting before making any changes. Similarly, cut all the grooves before resetting the rip fence for another operation. And cut all the tenons at the same time. Adjusting a frame after the joinery has been cut can be an enormous headache. It's easier to get it right the first time.

3. **Adjust the stop on your miter gauge** to cut the rails 4 in. shorter than the final width of the door. (This figure accounts for the ½-in. tenons that will go into the stiles minus the width of the stiles.)

4. **Cut a ½-in.-deep groove** down the length of each component with a ¼-in. dado blade in the tablesaw. (See p. 24 for how to set up a dado blade.) Flip each piece around and repeat the cut to ensure each groove is perfectly centered. (The blade won't recut if it's on center.) If not, adjust the rip fence so the groove is dead center.

5. **Set the saw fence to ½ in. from the outside of the blade** and raise the standard blade to just a hair beyond ¼ in.

6. **Score and define the tenon shoulders.**

7. **Set up a stacked dado blade,** and adjust it to be slightly narrower than the length of your tenon but not so wide as to rub the rip fence.

8. **Take a partial depth cut** of the tenon cheek on each side to test the height of the blade.

9. **Test the fit.** Adjust the height of the blade slowly, sneaking up on the perfect fit.

10. **Take a full cut,** riding the end of the tenon against the rip fence to stop the depth of the cut.

11. **Make a final test fit.**

workSmart

If you don't have a dado blade, you can use a standard blade to cut the grooves and tenons by nibbling up to the final cut. It's time-consuming, and you must be consistent in the process, especially with the final cut.

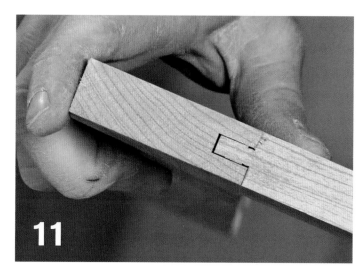

workSmart

Testing the fit of the tenon is critical to the success of the frame assembly. The tenon should fit snugly with hand pressure or a gentle tap. If you have to slam it home with a hammer, the stile may split on assembly, especially since the wood fibers will swell slightly after the glue is applied. Because the initial fitting is so important, keep your offcuts from cutting the rails and stiles for test-cutting the tenons until you get the joint just right.

Assembling a frame and panel

The strength of this stub-tenon frame and panel relies partly on the glued-in plywood panel. Plywood is dimensionally stable. Don't try this with a solid-wood panel, which will expand and contract throughout the seasons. Wood movement will literally tear your door apart. When gluing, remember that a little goes a long way. Avoid applying so much glue that your frame is dripping with squeeze-out. You'll just have more to clean up later.

1. **Dry-fit the frame assembly.** Measure the opening to size the panel. Add 1 in. to the height and width of the measurement for the panel.

2. **Cut a piece of ¼-in. plywood to this size.**

3. **Dry-fit the assembly.**

4. **Apply glue to the tenons** and along the bottom of the groove.

5. **Assemble the frame.**

6. **Clamp the frame** until the rail tenons fit snugly into the groove in the stiles.

7. **Check the assembly for square** by measuring across the diagonals. The frame is square when they're the same length.

> **workSmart**
>
> For a little extra insurance, you can always pin the joints from the back with a ⅝-in. brad.

Quick glass panel doors

I learned this method from Udo Schmidt. Make your frames as described on p. 89–91. Order the glass ½ in. wider than the opening. Before assembly, rip away the portion of wood defining the groove on the inside of the rails. Glue and assemble the frame and finish it. Apply a few dabs of clear silicone adhesive to the center of the rail. Slide the glass into frame and center it, then allow the silicone to cure.

Fitting an inset drawer front

Drawer fronts are attached *after* the drawer slides are installed (see Chapter 8). Whether the inset drawer front is a frame-and-panel assembly or solid wood, fitting it is essentially the same. The main difference is where the attachment screws are placed.

1. **Install the drawer slides** according to the manufacturer's directions and make sure they operate smoothly.

2. **Position ¹⁄₁₆-in. shims** under the drawer to hold it in the correct location for fastening. With your eye, adjust the drawer front side to side until the gaps are equal.

3. **Hold the drawer front** securely with one hand.

4. **Tack the drawer front** from behind to the drawer box with 1-in. staples. Drive screws from the inside of the front of the drawer box on the centerline if the drawer front is solid wood. If the drawer front has a frame, drive screws into the frame.

5. **Remove the shims and check the drawer operation.**

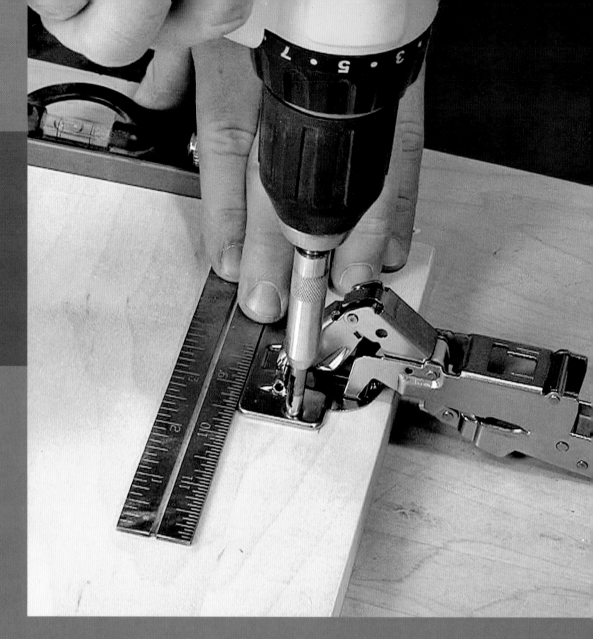

Installing hardware

ow that all of the cabinets are built, it's time to install the hardware that will make the doors and drawers functional. Although there are many choices for hinges and drawer runners, I usually reach for Euro-style hinges and full-extension drawer slides. They operate smoothly and are extremely durable. Because they're very adjustable, they're also easy to install.

The Euro-style 32 mm system of hardware, used in large cabinet shops, relies on a series of uniformly positioned holes, 32 mm apart from one another, set into the cabinet on a 37 mm centerline. In a small shop, the system can be used to line up hardware components such as hinges and drawer slides very efficiently, without the need for tedious figuring.

In this chapter, I'll discuss the choices in hardware. I'll also show you how to install side-mount, full-extension slides and easy-to-adjust cup hinges.

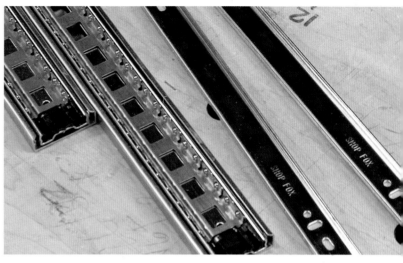

Modern drawer slides rely on ball bearings for their smooth operation. The slide can be separated into a cabinet section (left) and a drawer section (right) for easy installation.

Drawer slides

Cabinetmakers have many options when it comes to drawer hardware. Catalogs offer many brands, sizes, and styles. Despite the wide variety of choices, there is one type of slide that I use over and over again—the side-mount, full-extension slide. This type of slide meets the industry standard of supporting 100 lb. and actually operates more smoothly when bearing weight up to the rated maximum load.

Choices in mounting location

Side-mount, full-extension slides are easy to install, and I've never had a failure with them. Plus there's no complicated math to calculate when building drawer boxes. Slides of this type require ½ in. of space per side, so drawers are simply 1 in. narrower than the cabinet or face frame opening. Although 22 in. deep is standard for base cabinet drawers and pullouts, other lengths are available in 2-in. increments, usually from about 6 in. to 28 in. Enhanced versions of the basic slide offer options such as self-closing, soft-closing, and touch-open action.

Undermount slides take slightly less space and are nearly invisible after installation. They are more difficult to install and more expensive than side-mount slides.

Two styles of undermount slides. Nylon roller slides (left) are less expensive but not as durable as ball-bearing slides (right).

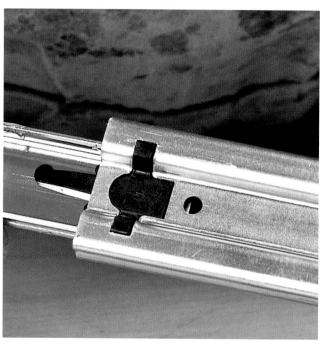

The two parts of the slide release by means of a tab or button.

Installing slides

Installing drawer slides begins by separating them into two parts. Some versions have little levers to accomplish this, while others have buttons. Generally speaking, the smaller part of the slide attaches to the drawer box.

For side-mount slides, the bottom of the drawer should be about ⅛ in. above the bottom edge of the slide assembly. I use a simple shopmade locating jig to position the slide on the drawer box at a consistent height of ⁵⁄₁₆ in. from the bottom edge. The front of the slide lines up with the front of the drawer box.

The larger portion of the slide attaches to the cabinet side. To position it, use a scrap of wood as a spacer, which will ensure that the slide is parallel to the cabinet's top or bottom. After installing the separate components, make sure the drawer runners fit into one another and slide in and out of the cabinet effortlessly.

In face-frame installations, you'll need to add a spacer to fill the gap between the cabinet side and the face frame so that the slide can fully extend without contacting the frame. I usually cut a strip of ¼-in. plywood to shim the slide to the right distance and finish it to match the

A simple jig made of scrap plywood makes it easy to position the slide exactly 5/16 in. above the bottom edge of the drawer side. You can also use the jig to steady the slide while you drill the pilot holes and drive the screws.

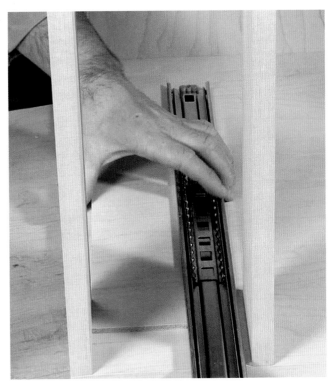

A block of wood or a piece of plywood helps position the slide on the cabinet interior, ensuring a consistent location.

On face-frame cabinets, shim out the slide with 1/4-in. plywood so that the slide can clear the face frame.

interior of the cabinet. If you've planned inset doors and drawers in your face-frame cabinets, make sure to line the slide up to the back edge of the frame to account for the thickness of the drawer front.

Once you've installed the drawer slides, you're ready to install drawer fronts. For information on building and installing drawer fronts, see Chapter 7.

workSmart

Some drawer slides come with screws and some don't. Check when you order the slides and make sure to get the right length for your drawers. A screw that's even a hair too long can penetrate the drawer box, leaving a sharp point on the outside. If this happens, use a shorter screw or place a #6 washer as a spacer. Just make sure the raised screw head doesn't interfere with the operation of the slide.

Like drawer slides, cup hinges come in a wide variety of styles for different applications.

The location of the cup bore is dictated by standard rules. The distance of the hinge from the top or bottom edge may vary. I usually position the hinge 3 in. o.c. from the top or the bottom edge.

Hinges

Euro-style, or cup, hinges come in many designs, allowing you to choose how far the door opens, as well as the amount of overlay or inset of the door. Despite the variety, the mechanics of installing them are pretty much the same.

Every door will require at least two hinges, and depending on the height or weight of the door, it may require more. My general rule of thumb is to use one hinge for every 15 in. to 18 in. of door height, so the average 30-in. (or shorter) door will only use two. To ensure long-term reliability, be sure to check with the hinge manufacturer to determine the right number of hinges for your door installation.

Converting metric hinge measure		
PURPOSE	**MM**	**IN.**
Door cup hinge-bore centerline	22.5	⁷⁄₈
Standard spacing for production-line boring	32	1¼
Diameter of hinge-cup bore	35	1³⁄₈
Setback for line boring—use to align hinge plates	37	1¹⁵⁄₃₂

A 35 mm Forstner bit mounted in a drill press is the easiest and fastest way to bore the flat-bottomed holes for cup hinges.

If you don't have a drill press, you can use a commercial hinge jig with a portable drill.

Installing the cup mechanism

The installation of Euro-style hinges starts at the drill press with a flat-bottomed hole drilled with a 35 mm Forstner bit. Most Euro-style hinges specify the location of the hinge cup at 22.5 mm, or ⅞ in., o.c. from the edge of the door. There's no set standard for the distance of the hinge from the top or bottom. I usually place mine 3 in. o.c. from the top and bottom edges. Make adjust-

ments to this dimension if the hinge placement will interfere with one of the pullouts in the cabinet.

Forstner bits work best at slow speeds, so adjust the drill press accordingly. Bore about ½ in. deep, but don't drill through the door completely. The exact depth can be calculated by measuring the height of the hinge cup. You can usually find this dimension specified in the hinge instructions.

If you don't have a drill press, there are specialty jigs available to complete this step. With practice, the hinge bore can be drilled successfully by hand, although it certainly takes more time.

workSmart

If you don't have a 35 mm bit, a 1⅜-in. Forstner bit will work in a pinch.

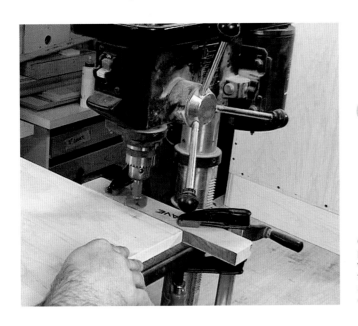

Clamp a fence to the drill press table so that the bit will consistently drill on the guideline. The fence also helps steady the door during drilling.

Use one of the hinge mounting plates as a drilling template. Use a #3 self-centering bit.

Installing the hinge mounting plate

For the case side of the hinge installation, it's best to lay the cabinet on the bench, hinge side down. Follow the manufacturer's instruction to lay out the location of the hinge. Set up an adjustable square to make accurate marks, usually 37 mm from the cabinet's front edge. This distance may vary depending on your hinge make and application, so double check. Next, line up the door against the cabinet face, open the hinge arms, and draw center marks on the cabinet at the ends of the hinge arms. Use a square to extend the marks to the front edge.

Line up the hinge mounting plate so the centerlines on the cabinet intersect the holes in the plate, and drill a couple pilot holes with a self-centering bit. Secure the plate with #6 by ⅝-in.-long screws. To wrap up installation, just clip the hinge arm to the mounting plate. Presto—a working door.

Accommodating pullouts

Even though your hinges may open to 90 degrees or more, the actual door itself protrudes into the cabinet space, making pullouts unusable. In order to accommodate this, you need to install hinges that will pivot the door out of the way. I use 170-degree hinges for this purpose. When fully opened, the door will completely clear the cabinet side, allowing the pullout to do its job.

But what if your cabinet is at the end of a run, butted against a wall or a refrigerator, and you can't open the cabinet door past 90 degrees? Well, you could hinge the door on the other side of the cabinet box. But if that's not an option, the solution may be a zero-protrusion hinge. Zero-protrusion, or zero-clearance, hinges usually are sold as 155- to 165-degree opening hinges, but these actually clear the side of the cabinet when they reach the 90-degree point.

Be sure to position the hinge so that it does not interfere with the operation of pullouts. You may need to use zero-clearance hinges in some installations.

Hinging face frame cabinets

Special face frame hinges are available, but they focus all of their mounting strength on the face frame itself. Long term, this isn't a very durable solution. Instead, I just shim the cabinets, and trick the hinge into thinking it's in a Euro-style cabinet. Be sure to mark the hinge plate location 37 mm from the back edge of the face frame instead of from the front edge of the cabinet . Also, since there's a ¼-in. gap, or reveal, between the opening of the face frame and the cabinet box, be sure to shim it with a spacer block. You can use small blocks of wood or a full-length strip from top to bottom. Just cut the shims large enough to support the mounting plates, and finish them to match the cabinet interior. Finally, you'll need to add a small stop block or strip of wood if using inset doors, so the door has a positive stop.

A block of wood raises the mounting plate flush to the face frame.

A block on the opposite side serves as a door stop.

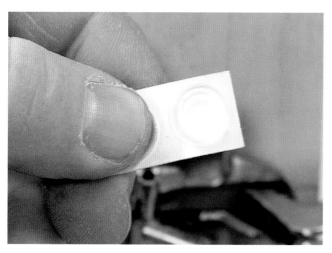

Self-stick rubber bumpers reduce noise and cushion the door when it closes.

The next step is hinge adjustment. Besides ease of installation, one of the biggest advantages of using Euro-style hinges is adjustability. Most hinges have the means to adjust the hinge and door assembly in every axis. So whether the door needs to go up, down, in, out, side to side, or even twisted around in a combination of the three axis, the correction is as simple as turning a screw.

Install accessories, including trim plates, magnetic catches, and bumpers after finishing. A simple and inexpensive way to prevent the door from slamming against the cabinet are clear self-stick bumpers.

Installing side-mount drawer slides

The installation of side-mount slides goes more smoothly when you use shopmade jigs to position the components.

1. **Separate the slides** into their two components by engaging the release mechanism.

2. **Use a spacer** to align the smaller portion of the slide to the drawer box.

3. **Align the front of the slide** to the front of the drawer box.

4. **Make sure the slide is flush** to the front with a scrap of wood placed on the front of the box. If the slide overhangs the front, it could interfere with installation of the drawer front.

5. **Drill pilot holes** using a #3 self-centering drill bit.

6. **Attach the slide to the drawer** with three or four screws.

workSmart

This spacer jig is nothing more than scrap ¼-in. plywood tacked to a strip of ¾-in. plywood. The overhang is exactly ⁵⁄₁₆ in. Make sure the two parts are straight to one another. Cut the strips on the tablesaw, and lay them on the spine of the jig to align them during nailing.

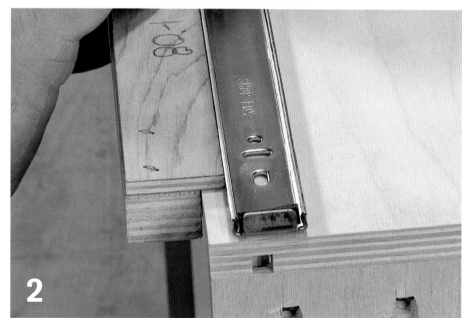

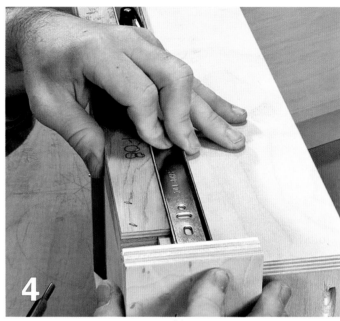

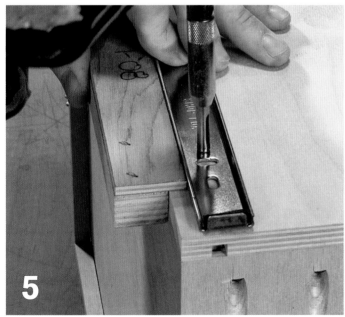

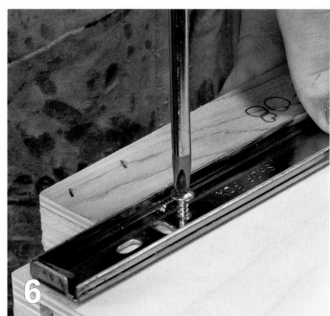

Installing side-mount drawer slides (continued)

7. **Put the slide together** to make sure it will operate without binding. Then take the slide apart and turn over the drawer. Install the drawer component on the opposite side of the drawer box as described in the previous steps.

8. **Position the larger portion of the slide to the cabinet.** Use a spacer to ensure parallel placement, and align it with the front edge of the cabinet (on frameless cabinets) or the back edge of the face frame.

9. **Drill pilot holes** for the screws using a #3 self-centering bit.

10. **Secure the slide** to the cabinet side with three or four screws.

11. **Slide the drawer box** into the cabinet, making sure the two slide components fit together and are aligned correctly.

12. **Test the operation** of the slides with the drawer in the cabinet.

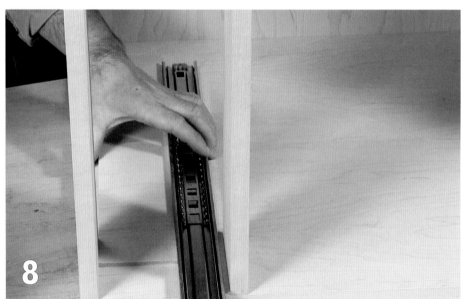

Installing cup hinges

The key to installing cup hinges is careful layout and alignment of the hinge arms with the plate. Use a sliding square to transfer measurements.

1. **Mark the distance** from the edge of the door according to the manufacturer's instructions.

2. **Use a sliding square to mark the center** of the cup hole. I usually locate the center 3 in. from the top or bottom edge.

3. **Clamp a fence to the drill press table** so that the point of the Forstner bit aligns with the vertical axis of the bore line.

4. **Drill until the bit reaches the set depth.**

5. **Clear any chips from the hole.** Double-check the depth and make any adjustments.

6. **Use a square to align the cup** and drill pilot holes with a self-centering bit.

7. **Mark the depth for the mounting plate,** usually 37 mm but check the manufacturer's specifications.

8. **Lay the door next to the cabinet.** Make sure the door is in the correct position for the planned overlay or inset. Mark the centerline of the hinge arm.

9. **Carry across the centerline** using a sliding square.

workSmart

Remember to run large Forstner bits at a slow speed and avoid overheating. You may need to clear the shavings from time to time.

10. **Line up the mounting plate** with the centerlines. Drill pilot holes with a self-centering bit. Partially drive the set screw before drilling all the holes to aid in holding the plate for drilling.

11. **Drive the screws.** Don't completely tighten them as the plate position may need adjustment.

12. **Clip hinge arms onto the mounting plates.**

13. **Make adjustments, if necessary,** by loosening the screws in the hinge plate and moving it up or down.

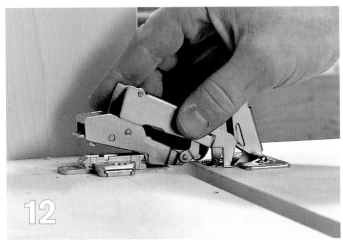

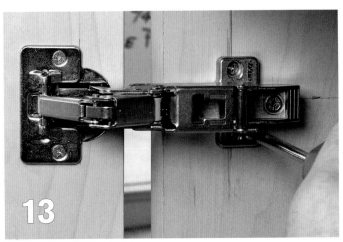

❯workSmart

Some fasteners on Euro-style hinges my look like Phillips® head screws, but the extra little X-shaped marking gives away their true identity. These screws should be worked only with a Pozidriv® screwdriver. Pozidriv screws have a slightly different internal shape, and using a standard Phillips driver with them may cause the head to strip out. Most hinge suppliers and hardware suppliers carry Pozidriv screwdrivers for just a few dollars.

Installing hardware in face-frame cabinets

Installing drawer slides and hinges in face-frame cabinets is simply a matter of raising the hardware so that it clears the frame. Generally, ¼-in.-thick strips of plywood or solid wood will work to shim drawer slides and hinges to the proper height. The actual thickness you need depends on the hardware manufacturer's specifications.

1. **Tack a ¼-in.-thick strip** of plywood or solid wood as wide as the drawer slide and long enough to accommodate the length of the component.

2. **Position the slide,** taking into account the setback dictated by the face-frame thickness, and drill pilot holes.

3. **Secure the slide with screws.**

4. **Nail blocks on the cabinet wall** to support the hinge mounting plates and as a door stop.

5. **Install cup hinges** as shown on pp. 108–110.

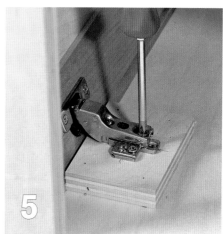

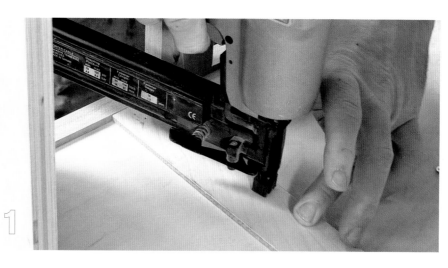

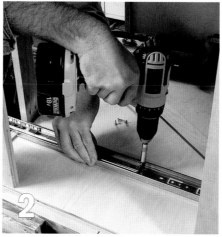

Finishing

The transformation from simple boxes to cabinets is nearly complete, but there are a few more steps before wrapping things up, starting with the application of a durable finish. The finish will bring out the beauty of natural wood as well as protecting the cabinet from water and household detergents. I've come up with a simple finishing method that's nearly foolproof and provides good protection for your cabinets. In this chapter, I'll share my not-so-secret recipe and the easy steps to applying it. You'll also need to install hardware to open and close the cabinets. Fortunately, installation is pretty simple, especially with commercial or shopmade jigs.

Choosing a finish

Kitchens are a harsh environment, where grease, water, and aggressive cleaners can damage cabinets. The finish you choose must be able to resist all these. There are many options for finishing cabinets. Transparent finishes include shellac, varnish, polyurethane, and other solvent-based finishes. In the last 20 years, water-based versions of these traditional finishes have also become available. They are slightly less durable but offer fast cleanup with water. Paint has been used to finish kitchen cupboards for hundreds of years. It comes in an infinite variety of colors and can be worked with tools and other materials to create interesting surface effects.

Transparent or natural finishes

The warmth of wood becomes even more attractive when coated with a transparent finish. Finishes darken the natural color of the wood and bring out the grain. Highly figured woods like bird's-eye maple or curly cherry really show their beauty only once they've been finished.

Shellac is a traditional clear finish that dries quickly. Since the solvent for shellac is alcohol, shellac isn't the best choice for a kitchen, where you may spill alcoholic beverages. Traditional varnishes are fairly thick and hard to brush out. They often take a long time to dry, during which dust can settle in the finish. My finish of choice is

Finishing doesn't need to be complicated. You can mix your own wipe-on finish with a few widely available ingredients. Always remember to wear personal safety equipment, including nitrile gloves and a respirator when working with solvent-borne finishes like oil-based polyurethane.

oil-based polyurethane. It can be too thick right out of the can, so I mix it with a solvent and linseed oil. That way I can wipe it on rather than brush it. It dries more quickly applied in a thin layer, eliminating the problem of dust in the finish.

Paint

Paint used for kitchens should be as durable as possible. Gloss and semigloss sheens resist stains and wipe clean more easily than flat-sheen paints. There are many decorative effects possible with paints. Kits are available to provide all the materials you'll need. Some paint effects need a clear-coat finish on top of them to protect the surface from damage in a kitchen.

Solvent borne vs. water based

Solvent-borne finishes impart a warm look to natural wood. They also emit fumes dangerous to your lungs, so always use them in a well-ventilated space and use appropriate safety equipment. Water-based finishes are now available for nearly every conceivable type of finish, even shellac. Water-based finishes clean up with water

and emit fewer toxic chemicals, but they're also less durable. They also have a bluish tinge and lack the warmth of oil-based finishes. Some states have banned finishes that give off VOCs (volatile organic compounds) for the sake of air quality. If you live in one of those states, a water-based finish may be your only option.

Choosing knobs and pulls

There are knobs and pulls to suit every style and taste. Many decorative finishes are available, enabling you to create an accurate period style, or you can choose sleek contemporary designs. Whatever hardware you choose, make sure it is well made and durable. Knobs and pulls get a lot of hard use in a kitchen.

Be sure to get the right length screws for the hardware. If you're installing knobs or pulls on drawers with an applied drawer front, you'll need to consider the thickness of the drawer box, usually ½ in. Most hardware comes with screws meant for ¾-in. material, so you'll need to purchase longer screws for drawers with applied drawer fronts.

Pulls require two holes for installation, whereas knobs require only one. On very wide drawers, it's advisable to use two pulls or knobs for visual balance as well as ease of operation.

Preparing surfaces for finishing

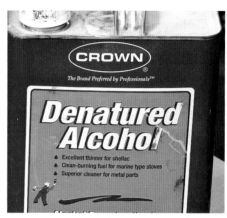

Use denatured alcohol to clean up fingerprints, dirt, chalk, and pencil marks before sanding.

Good surface preparation always tells in the final result. The reverse is also true. Remove stains, oil, and glue before sanding. Don't skimp on sanding—get as much dust off the surface as possible before finishing.

1. **Wipe down all of the cabinet surfaces** with alcohol or mineral spirits to remove any contaminants that could interfere with finish adhesion. The wipe down helps remove pencil marks and some stains. Fill any voids with matching wood putty compatible with the finish you're using.

2. **Sand thoroughly.** Begin sanding bare wood with 100-grit sandpaper. On plywood, start the sanding sequence at 150-grit sandpaper to avoid cutting through the thin veneer faces.

3. **Use compressed air or a vacuum to remove the sanding dust** and grit between each stage of sanding. Continue sanding through successive grits until you reach 180-grit sandpaper.

warning

Always wear an effective dust mask when sanding to protect your lungs.

Making a wipe-on finish

O il-based polyurethane used right from the can is thick and slow to dry. I like to thin it to make it more workable. By diluting it with paint thinner and adding some oil, you can make a very effective wipe-on finish, commonly known as 3:2:1, which refers to the ratio of the ingredients. Use a graduated mason jar to get the ratio just right. Make as much of this finish as you can use in a day or so, mixing more as you need it.

warning

Work in a well-ventilated area whenever working with a solvent-borne finish to protect your lungs. For extra protection, wear a cartridge mask designed to filter out harmful fumes.

1. **Pour 3 parts paint thinner or mineral spirits** into a graduated glass jar.

2. **Add 2 parts polyurethane.**

3. **Add 1 part boiled linseed oil.** Pure tung oil can be substituted and offers a little extra moisture resistance.

4. **Screw the lid on the jar tightly.** Shake vigorously to mix well. Don't worry about bubbles in this finish—the wet-sanding method we'll use will eliminate them.

warning

Avoid using electric sanders when applying 3:2:1. The finish contains flammable liquid and vapors. Sparks from the sander motor could start a fire or create an explosion.

Applying a wipe-on finish

Wipe-on finishes, like 3:2:1, really lend themselves to the home shop environment because of their ease of application. It's a simple yet durable finish. Sanding while the finish is wet and wiping off the slurry prevents dust or debris from getting stuck in the top coat while drying. Because 3:2:1 is a thin finish, I put a minimum of four coats on all the cabinet surfaces, but you may want to apply additional coats on heavy-wear surfaces like drawer fronts.

1. **Flood the workpiece with finish** using a disposable foam brush or rag. Don't worry about even coverage; just generously apply the finish to the wood.

2. **Sand the wet finish into the wood** with abrasive pads or 400-grit wet/dry sandpaper. As you sand, a light sanding slurry will develop. This will help fill the grain for a smoother surface.

3. **Wipe off the excess finish** and allow the workpiece to dry. The initial coat of finish may take a day or so to dry. Apply a second coat just like the first, but use lighter pressure when sanding. Light scuff sanding of the wet finish on subsequent coats will knock down any raised grain or dust. Additional coats usually dry in as little as 3 to 4 hours, depending on the temperature and humidity. Oil finishes cure slowly and will emit vapors for some time. Leave any finished cabinets or drawers open and exposed in a well-ventilated area while curing to prevent the buildup of unpleasant odors.

> **warning**
>
> Wet rags used for solvents and oil finishes, such as 3:2:1, pose a fire hazard as they dry, especially balled up in container. Spread them out, preferably outside, and allow them to dry thoroughly before disposing.

Installing knobs on doors

Installing knobs or pulls for the doors and drawer fronts is the last step in cabinet construction. The typical location of a knob on a door is about one-third of the way down from the top of the door for base cabinets and the reverse for wall cabinets. I like to locate mine closer to the nearest open corner of the door, where they're handier to reach.

1. **Use a jig to lay out the location** for the screw hole. This helps ensure that placement is consistent and uniform throughout the entire project. Drill through the door with a bit just larger than the screws (typically ³⁄₁₆ in.). A backer block of scrapwood clamped behind where the hole will be drilled helps eliminate tearout when the drill exits the back of the door.

2. **Insert the screw from the back.**

3. **Hold the screw from the back** and twist on the knob. Tighten lightly with a screwdriver. Don't overtighten!

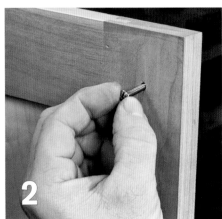

Installing knobs on drawer fronts

Installing knobs on drawer fronts is essentially the same as for doors, except that knobs for drawers are usually centered.

1. **Find the centerline of the drawer.**

2. **Use a jig to lay out the location** for the screw hole.

3. **Hold the screw from the back** and twist on the knob. Tighten lightly with a screwdriver.

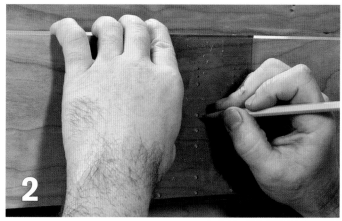

Installing pulls

Pulls install like knobs except there are two screw holes to drill. Create a template to mark out the location of the holes and drill them on the drill press before attaching the drawer front. For doors, you can make a jig to guide the drill similar to the one shown in step 1 on the facing page.

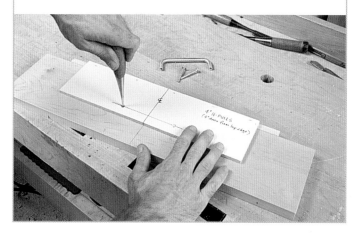

resources

For tools, cabinet hardware, pocket screw jigs

- **Lee Valley® Tools**
  From US: (800) 871-8158
  From Canada: (800) 267-8767
  www.leevalley.com

- **McFeely's™**
  (800) 443-7937
  www.mcfeelys.com

- **Rockler® Woodworking and Hardware**
  (800) 279-4441
  www.rockler.com

- **Woodcraft®**
  (800) 535-4486
  www.woodcraft.com

- **Woodworker's Hardware®**
  (800) 383-0130
  www.wwhardware.com

- **Woodworker's Supply®**
  (800) 645-9292
  www.woodworker.com

Further reading

- **All New Kitchen Idea Book**
  Joanne Kellar Bouknight
  The Taunton Press, Inc.

- **Building Doors and Drawers**
  Andy Rae
  The Taunton Press, Inc.

- **Building Kitchen Cabinets**
  Udo Schmidt
  The Taunton Press, Inc.

- **Building Traditional Kitchen Cabinets**
  Jim Tolpin
  The Taunton Press, Inc.

- **Build Your Own Kitchen Cabinets**
  Danny Proulx
  Popular Woodworking Books

- **Great Wood Finishes**
  Jeff Jewitt
  The Taunton Press, Inc.

- **Kitchens for the Rest of Us**
  Peter Lemos
  The Taunton Press, Inc.

- **Kitchen Ideas that Work**
  Beth Veillette
  The Taunton Press, Inc.

- **The New Woodfinishing Book**
  Michael Dresdner
  The Taunton Press, Inc.

- **Painting and Finishing**
  Michael Dresdner
  The Taunton Press, Inc.

- **Taunton's Complete Illustrated Guide to Choosing and Installing Hardware**
  Bob Settich
  The Taunton Press, Inc.

- **Taunton's Complete Illustrated Guide to Furniture and Cabinetmaking**
  Andy Rae
  The Taunton Press, Inc.

- **Taunton's Complete Illustrated Guide to Joinery**
  Gary Rogowski
  The Taunton Press, Inc.

- **Taunton's Complete Illustrated Guide to Routers**
  Lonnie Bird
  The Taunton Press, Inc.

- **Taunton's Complete Illustrated Guide to Tablesaws**
  Paul Anthony
  The Taunton Press, Inc.

Other resources

- **Architectural Woodwork Institute**
  46179 Westlake Dr.
  Suite 120
  Potomac Falls, VA 20165
  www.awinet.org

- **Kitchen Cabinet Manufacturers Association (KCMA®)**
  1899 Preston White Dr.
  Reston, VA 20191-5435
  www.kcma.org

- **True32 Flow Manufacturing**
  Bob Buckley
  www.true32.com

index